IMAGES
of America

ROAN MOUNTAIN

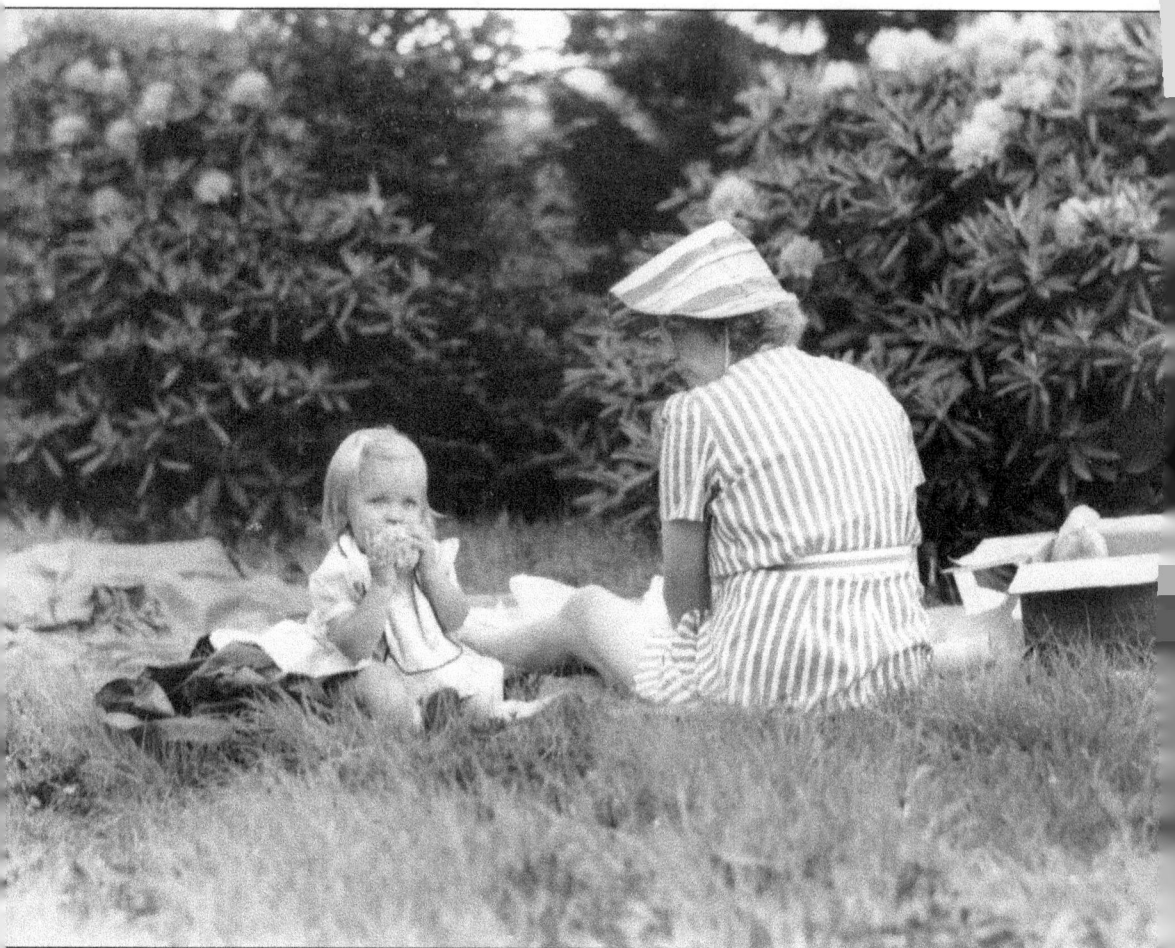

ON THE ROAN. Young Linda Behrend is pictured here enjoying an orange for the first time as she rests on a blanket. Linda took this trip to the top of Roan Mountain in the summer of 1946 with her mother, Mary Fern Green Behrend, and her father, Fred Behrend. Decades later, she recalled that her parents attempted to take the orange from her, but she would not let go. (Courtesy of Linda Behrend.)

ON THE COVER: The Cloudland High School band, directed by Gene Proffitt, is seen here in 1955 performing during the Rhododendron Festival on top of Roan Mountain. The festival featured entertainment, food, speeches, and a beauty pageant. It was held on the top of the mountain near the famous Rhododendron Gardens. The festival eventually moved to Roan Mountain State Park. (Courtesy of Tennessee State Archives and Library.)

IMAGES
of America

ROAN MOUNTAIN

Robert Sorrell
Foreword by Chandrea Street Shell

ARCADIA
PUBLISHING

Published by Arcadia Publishing
Charleston, South Carolina

Library of Congress Control Number: 2013956755

For all general information, please contact Arcadia Publishing:
Telephone 843-853-2070
Fax 843-853-0044
E-mail sales@arcadiapublishing.com
For customer service and orders:
Toll-Free 1-888-313-2665

Visit us on the Internet at www.arcadiapublishing.com

For my family and friends, who have supported me during this project.

CONTENTS

FOREWORD

In the shadow of one of the Appalachian Mountains' most notable peaks lies a community rich in history and strong in faith.

The stunning highland vistas, flora, and fauna that greeted Roan Mountain's first inhabitants continue to embrace and intrigue residents and visitors today. The grassy balds and native Catawba Rhododendron Gardens atop Roan Mountain, as well as the town's crown jewel, Roan Mountain State Park, bring thousands of visitors to the area each year. But beyond the area's natural beauty is a body of genuine, assiduous people with intrinsic Southern hospitality that entices many visitors each year to call this beloved area home.

Numerous descendants of those who saw the East Tennessee & Western North Carolina Railroad, affectionately referred to as the "Tweetsie," pass through town or greeted the prestigious visitors of General Wilder's hotels continue to call Roan Mountain home. Others choose to worship, work, and live in a community where neighbors help neighbors, strangers soon become friends, and the seasons magically unfold before them.

This book beautifully chronicles the fascinating history of Roan Mountain, preserving our community's rich heritage for generations to come. Many thanks to Robert Sorrell for his diligence in pulling together a pictorial masterpiece that captures the essence of the community, as well as the heart of its people!

To the countless individuals who rummaged through old photograph boxes and albums to provide important pieces of history, your efforts are appreciated. To those who recalled stories and moments that weaved together this historical tapestry, we are forever grateful. Most importantly, to the many homes this book showcases, our most cherished treasures, we are thankful for the community you helped establish for all to enjoy.

May each of us leave our community and our world better off than we found it.

—Chandrea Street Shell

ACKNOWLEDGMENTS

This Roan Mountain history book would not have been possible without the support and assistance of former and current residents. I am grateful to the countless contributors of photographs, historical documents, factual information, and personal stories about Roan Mountain.

Contributors have included, in no particular order, Durward Julian and family, Dillard Street and family, Linda Brinkley Morgan, Patsy Young Crum, Julia Kodak, Esta Street Stevens, Fred Behrend's daughter Linda Behrend, Martha Whaley, Pam Watson Braswell, Andy Potter, Joanna Ledford Miller, the Floyd Hayes collection, Floyd Odom, Suzanne Tucker, the Robert Morgan family, Jeannie Perkins, Audrey Harrison Edney, Carter County Bank branch manager Brian Tipton, Jackie and Dawn Peters, Jack's Grocery, Jennifer Bauer, Jo Buchanan, John and Phyllis Orr, Johnny Blankenship, Judy Guinn, Juanita Wilson, Jennifer Fleenor Sizemore, Peggy Tipton Hershey, the Graybeal family, Karen Julian, Bob's Dairyland owner Joe Miller, Harvey Norris, Milligan College Archives, the Tennessee State Library and Archives, the North Carolina Archives, Bill Whitehead and family, Rebekah Hunt, Greg Whitehead, Ruth Barnett, J.L. Troutman and family, Dr. Rose Wolflin, Linda Perry Buchanan, Gary Stocton and family, Keith Hart, and the Cy Crumley collection. Jeannie Pippin Grizzard contributed several photographs in memory of the Pippin, Ledford, Harrison, Potter, and Grant families.

I want to especially thank Durward Julian and his daughter Vista Julian Clark for their 24-hour assistance. Former publisher Mark Stevens and the staff of the *Elizabethton Star* have also provided support, assistance, and workspace during this project.

INTRODUCTION

Roan Mountain, a scenic 6,285-foot peak in the southern Appalachian Mountains, one of the highest in the eastern United States, is located along the Tennessee–North Carolina border. Towering above quiet, historical, rural communities, the Roan features the world's largest natural rhododendron gardens, the longest grassy balds in the eastern United States, thick, record-breaking fir tree forests, the highest shelter along the Appalachian Trail, and a natural biosphere second to none.

Thousands of people have visited the Roan over the last two centuries, including European explorers, botanists, industrialists, and tourists. Native Americans were the first to visit Roan Mountain. Legend has it that a great battle was fought atop the Roan, but no evidence has been found to prove the tale. A few Native American artifacts, however, have been recovered from the mountain. Beginning in the 18th century, several notable explorers crossed the Roan to study its unique biology, including Andre Michaux, John Fraser, Elisha Mitchell, Asa Gray, and John Muir. Each traveler explored the Roan's spectacular natural wonders, identifying several new plants.

Early pioneers, including the Shell, Whitehead, Jones, Smith, and Oak families, began settling at the base and on the slopes of Roan Mountain in the late 18th century and early 19th century. The community remained isolated until shortly after the Civil War.

Following the Civil War, in the late 1860s, industrialists began scouring the Roan for natural resources. By 1875, the Crab Orchard Iron Company, owned and operated by three brothers from Crab Orchard, Tennessee, began operating mines along veins of the Cranberry (North Carolina) Mine. In Roan Mountain, the company established the Peg Leg Mine, which was located in what is now Roan Mountain State Park.

The East Tennessee & Western North Carolina Railroad, known by local residents as the "Tweestie," reached Roan Mountain in 1883 to haul iron away for further production. Once the railroad constructed a depot in the village, Roan Mountain's population began to grow. The railroad connected Roan Mountain with Johnson City in Tennessee and Boone in North Carolina. Railroad spurs connected the mines with the main tracks.

Civil War general John T. Wilder, an industrialist from Indiana, came to Roan Mountain in the 1880s. Wilder was interested in the area's burgeoning iron industry, but he also cashed in on the tourism industry. By 1884, he had built the Roan Mountain Inn along the Doe River, a few hundred feet from the new railroad depot. The general also constructed the popular Cloudland Hotel on top of the Roan. The Cloudland, which was first constructed of logs and was later a clapboard building, became a haven for wealthy tourists and international dignitaries. People with hay fever and other allergies sought the hotel's high altitude for relief.

Visitors would regularly stay and rest at the Roan Mountain Inn for a couple days before traveling by hack to the Cloudland Hotel. Hack drivers, including future railroad engineer Sherman Pippin, would take guests and supplies up the dirt hack line road in the morning and back down to the village in the afternoon. Many local residents tell stories about their grandparents and great-grandparents supplying food and services to the two hotels. The Cloudland Hotel had closed by 1920, but the Roan Mountain Inn remained open until at least 1950. Both buildings have since been demolished. The hack line road has been upgraded to a paved state highway.

Other businesses also opened in the village along Main Street, including the S.B. Wood Drug Store, which opened in 1898, and Robert Slaughter's Roan Mountain Theatre, which opened in the 1940s. Pierce Julian's general store was one of the first businesses in Roan Mountain. His store opened in 1893 and continued in operation for about 50 years. Julian's store was located near the drugstore, which still stands today as the oldest pharmacy in Tennessee.

Julian delivered a speech in 1919 to the Traveler's Protective Association in Bristol. In the speech, titled "Why I Live in Roan Mountain," Julian said, "Here lofty mountains lift their mighty peaks, ribbed with iron and granite, veined with coal and marble . . . covered with timbers rare in beauty and fine texture." He continued:

> Here it is the sun kisses the hilltops of sunny Tennessee, and here a thousand springs, clear as crystal and as cold as ice, burst from the earth and rivers are born. Deep down a thousand mossy glens, overshadowed with fir and hemlock, where the cataracts roar and splash, is found the fern and the galax, and the rhododendron and the leucothoe, while on a thousand hilltops the laurel and the azalea blush and blossom in wild profusion. I first saw the light of day in a rude log cabin beneath the shadows of the great Roan Mountain, more than six thousand feet above the level of the sea, upon whose summit I have stood when a barefoot boy and gazed out over an area of fifty thousand square miles.

Local residents nicknamed Julian the "Sage of Roan Mountain," as he was a noted communicator, advisor, and leader. Many people came to his store for advice about various life events.

In addition to Julian's store, Roan Mountain village also had a shoe cobbler, hardware stores, grocery stores, restaurants, mills, and a bank. In addition, there was a pipe factory, an herb and root warehouse, and a flooring facility. Centuries-old homes, including the historical Wilder House, can be found today in the village. Several historical churches, such as Roan Mountain United Methodist Church and Magill Memorial Presbyterian Church, are also in the village. A high school and elementary school have also opened.

Smaller communities developed around the village, including Shell Creek, Buck Mountain, Burbank, Cove Creek, Hampton Creek, Heaton Creek, Crabtree, Tiger Valley, Tiger Creek, and Ripshin. Each community has been home to schools, churches, stores, post offices, and residences. The Roan is within sight of each community.

The railroad, which followed the path of present-day US Highway 19E, ceased operations through Roan Mountain in the 1950s. The depot at Roan Mountain village, as well as the depots at nearby Shell Creek and Hopson, closed and were eventually demolished. Several rural schools and post offices have also closed and merged with the village.

In 1947, the citizens of Roan Mountain, Tennessee, and Bakersville, North Carolina, began holding the Rhododendron Festival. For years, thousands of residents would drive to the top of the mountain to enjoy food, entertainment, speeches, pageants, and the spectacular blooms of the rhododendron gardens. By 1958, the festival hit its peak. Local media estimated that nearly 100,000 people from around the country visited Roan Mountain, in part because of Vice Pres. Richard Nixon's visit.

The Rhododendron Festival was eventually taken off the mountain and is now held at Roan Mountain State Park, which officially opened in the 1970s. Situated between Roan Mountain village and the Burbank community, at the base of the mountain, the park allows visitors to enjoy hiking, swimming, camping, and scenic views. Pioneer David Miller's homestead sits within the park's boundaries, on Strawberry Mountain. The historical home and farm are open to the public.

Throughout the 20th century, visitors discovered Roan Mountain's unique natural beauty. In the 1930s and 1940s, East Tennessee State College professor D.M. Brown studied the mountain's biology. He regularly brought students to his mountaintop cabin to study the natural vegetation, as well as the results of lumber industry projects. The professor's cabin has been dismantled except for a remaining chimney, which now sits along the Appalachian Trail. Every day, curious hikers pass the chimney, located within two miles of the Cloudland Hotel site, the Rhododendron Gardens, the scenic Roan High Bluff, and the site of the former Roan High Knob Tower.

While visiting Roan Mountain in 1898, explorer John Muir wrote a letter to his wife about his journey. He wrote, "We drove here from Cranberry yesterday, a distance of about 18 miles through the most beautiful deciduous forest I ever saw. All the landscapes in every direction are made up of mountains, a billowing sea of them without bounds as far as one can look, and every mountain hill and ridge and hollow is densely forested with so many kinds of trees their mere names would fill this sheet and now they are beginning to put on their purple and gold."

Like every explorer before him and since, Muir was enchanted by the Roan's natural beauty. He also wrote about the lack of trees on the Roan's highest balds and the "glorious show" of the rhododendron gardens.

No one knows the origin of the Roan's name. Some say the reddish color, or "roan," of the rhododendron may be the story behind the mountain's name. Other locals, however, say it is named after Daniel Boone's roan-colored horse. Boone and his horse were frequent visitors to the mountain. The truth behind the Roan's name will likely never be known.

Elizabethton newspaperman Fred Behrend, a German immigrant born in 1896, fell in love with the Roan. His daughter Linda Behrend said her father compared the Roan to Germany's Black Forest. Behrend came to Elizabethton in 1926 to work at the rayon plants as a stenographer, but he later became a reporter and editor at the *Elizabethton Star*. He would take a few hours out of his day to break from the news beat and hike the Roan, enjoying its unique wildlife and flowers.

In 1959, Behrend, known as the "Bird Man," organized the first Carter County Wildflower Tour and Bird Walk, a predecessor of the Naturalists' Rally. The rallies continue to be held twice a year. Behrend became an honorary Roan Mountain resident and took part in the Roan Mountain Citizens Club and the Rhododendron Festival. He was an avid photographer and took hundreds of photographs of the Roan from the 1940s until he died in 1976. Many of those photographs, showing the mountain's natural wonders and visitors, are featured in this book.

One

ROAN MOUNTAIN

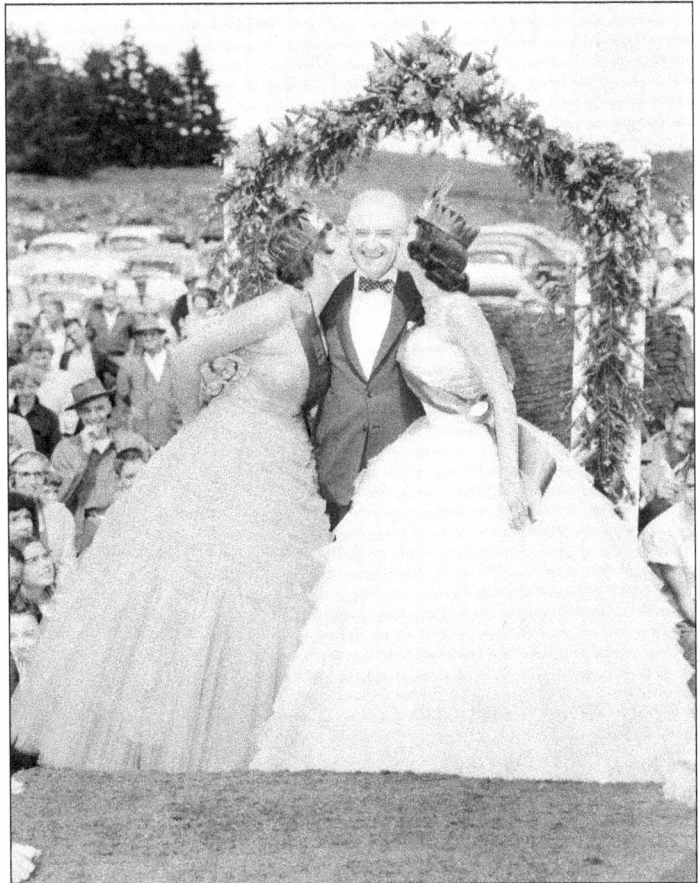

QUEENS KISS OFFICIAL. Joan Denton (left), Miss Rhododendron for Tennessee, and North Carolina's queen, Diane Rowland, kiss conservation commissioner Jim Nance McCord during the 1955 Rhododendron Pageant on top of Roan Mountain. Thousands attended the nationally recognized annual event beginning with the first pageant in 1948. (Courtesy of Tennessee State Library and Archives.)

CLOUDLAND HOTEL. The Cloudland Hotel, a haven for hay fever sufferers, was originally constructed as a 20-room spruce log lodge in the late 1870s on top of Roan Mountain. By 1885, Gen. John Wilder built a larger, three-story hotel a few hundred feet away. For one year, as seen in this rare photograph, both buildings stood on top of the mountain. The hack line, a dirt road from the village to the top of Roan, can also be seen in this picture. The hotel straddled the Tennessee–North Carolina state line and attracted dignitaries and wealthy guests from around the world. Guests could view 100 mountain peaks from the hotel. Local residents supported the hotel, as they would go up the hack line to take the staff and guests food and supplies. The popularity of the hotel decreased, and Wilder eventually was unable to operate the resort. It closed by the late 1910s. (Courtesy of Jackie and Dawn Peters.)

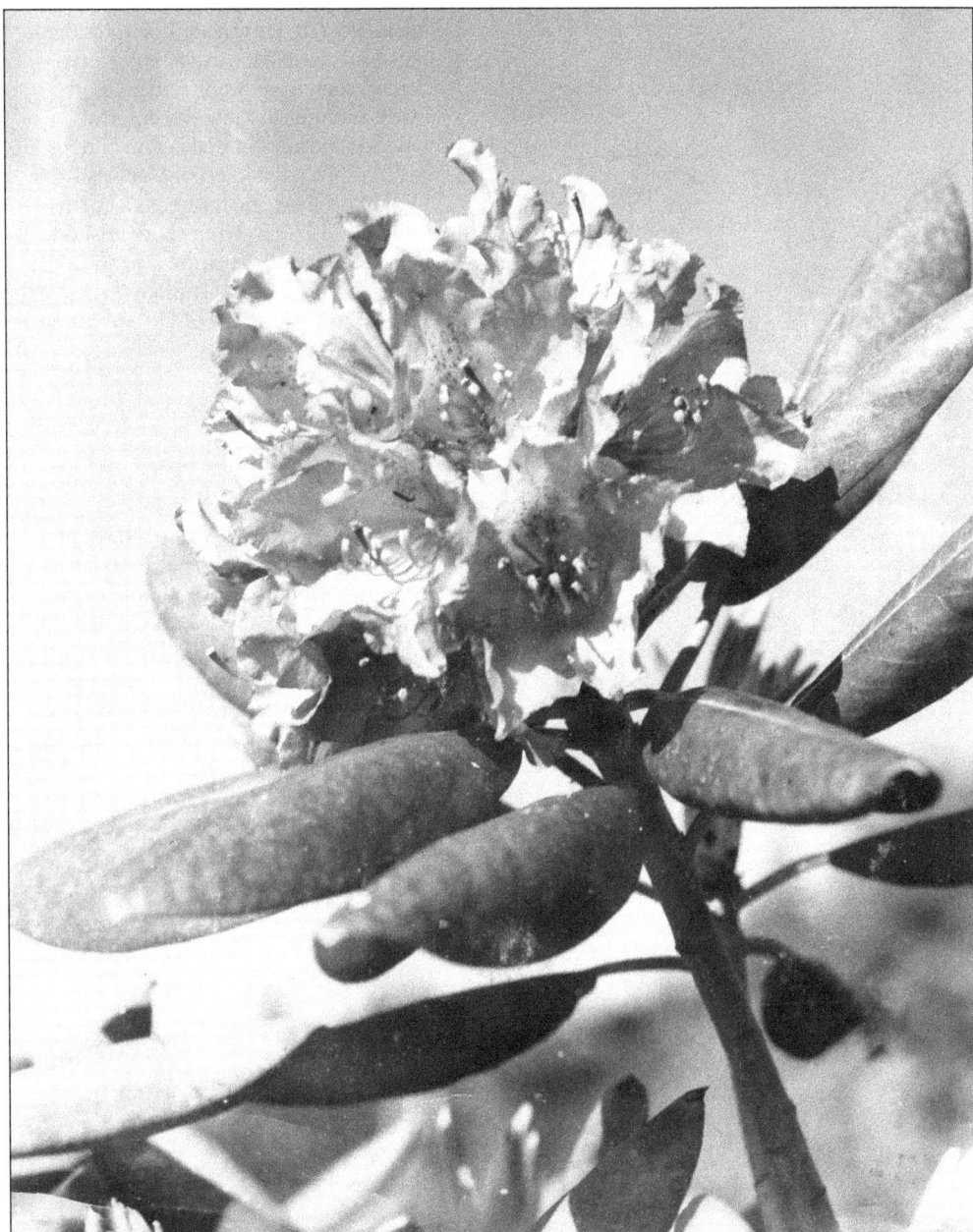

THE CATAWBA RHODODENDRON. The beautiful Catawba rhododendron plant flourishes on Roan Mountain. The peak is home to the world's largest natural rhododendron garden. Each June, thousands of people from around the world flock to the top of the Roan to view hundreds of crimson bushes in full bloom, which create a wonderland for photographers and flower enthusiasts. Photographer Fred Behrend captured this Catawba rhododendron around 1950. The large colorful plants, featuring big, dark-green leaves, spread several feet wide and high. A single bush in full bloom, generally in mid-June, can feature more than 100 crimson-colored flowers. The unique flowers have brilliant streaks and markings. The Catawba rhododendron is the highlight of the Roan, but other unique plants also live on the mountain. The Gray's lily is another unique Roan flower. (Courtesy of Linda Behrend.)

VISITING THE GARDENS. Local residents, such as Louise McKinney and Karen Street, seen here, went to the Roan every summer to view the colorful Rhododendron Gardens. The famous gardens are located off of Carvers Gap Road near the former site of the Cloudland Hotel. From there, visitors have access to the nearby Appalachian Trail, the Cloudland Trail, and the Roan High Bluff. (Courtesy of Dillard Street.)

CARS ON THE ROAN. Visitors have been traveling to the top of the Roan for centuries. By June 1940, people began arriving by automobile, as seen here. To reach the top, they had to drive up in the morning on a narrow dirt road. The one-way, gated road was reversed later in the afternoon so drivers could go down the mountain. (Courtesy of Tennessee State Library and Archives.)

ON THE BALDS. The Roan Highlands consist of several grassy and barren balds. The most recognized barren lands include Jane Bald, Round Bald, and Grassy Ridge Bald, which are some of the highest and largest balds in the Appalachian Mountains. The young boys in this photograph are hiking with their dog on one of the Roan's balds, which have captivated botanists for centuries because of their lack of trees. Dr. D.M. Brown, an East Tennessee State College botanist, planted a grove of fir trees on Round Bald to study their growth. The patch of trees can still be seen on the bald. Grassy Ridge Bald, with an elevation of 6,189 feet, is one of the highest balds in the Appalachians. There are several hundred acres of barren land on Grassy Ridge Bald. A plaque has been installed on its summit in honor of mountain farmer Cornelius Rex Peake, who supported the protection of the Roan. (Courtesy of Linda Behrend.)

ROAN HIGH BLUFF. The 6,267-foot Roan High Bluff, a rock outcropping accessible by the Cloudland Trail, has captivated visitors for centuries. The bluff is actually the second-highest point on Roan Mountain, after the Roan High Knob. Visitors do not have access to the highest point on the bluff, but can visit the overlook to take in the breathtaking views. Prior to the construction of a wooden deck, visitors had to climb onto the rocks to take in the view of the valley and other mountain peaks. This photograph was taken in the summer of 1939, long before the wooden deck was constructed. Even with the deck, visitors have a 180-degree view from the bluff, which is entirely located within the state of North Carolina, in Pisgah National Forest. (Courtesy of Tennessee State Library and Archives.)

FROZEN RHODODENDRONS. This strikingly beautiful photograph, taken by Fred Behrend, a naturalist and lover of Roan Mountain, features frozen rhododendron bushes. According to the back of the photograph, Behrend captured this image shortly after a dangerous winter storm had coated the mountain with a layer of ice. Old-timers would say the Roan was "frozen down" after these relatively frequent winter ice storms. (Courtesy of Linda Behrend.)

WINTER WONDERLAND. Snow covers Roan Mountain in this photograph. During the winter months, the 6,285-foot mountain receives several feet of snow, resulting in limited access to the top. Here, two people hike their way up the mountain on a dangerous snow- and ice-covered road. The photograph also shows the Roan's beautiful coniferous forests. (Courtesy of Linda Behrend.)

HIGH KNOB FIRE TOWER.
A small log cabin is
all that remains of the
former Roan High Knob
Fire Tower. In 1933, the
Civilian Conservation
Corps constructed the
tower atop Roan Mountain.
Although it was Tennessee's
highest tower, its location
was useless. Thick clouds
shrouded the structure,
creating low visibility. The
warden's cabin remains
intact and is used as an
Appalachian Trail shelter.
The Dellinger family is
seen in the photograph
above. They are, from
left to right, (first row)
Wayne and Jack Dellinger;
(second row) Rachel Lyons,
John Edwards, and James,
Sude, baby Jerry, and Bea
Dellinger. (Above, courtesy
of the Morgan family; left,
courtesy of Tennessee State
Library and Archives.)

STUDENTS VISIT THE ROAN. Students and staff at nearby Milligan College organized the Buffalo Ramblers, a hiking, walking, and exploring club. Clinton Holloway, a college historian, said the group regularly has excursions to Buffalo Mountain and Roan Mountain. In 1946, the club went to the top of the Roan. In the photograph above, from left to right, Bill Stanfield, Joe Hagan, Hugh "Doc" Thompson, and Thompson's two sons rest on a bluff. Below, from left to right, Hagan, Thompson, Don Pearce, Thompson's two sons, and Stanfield are seen at a campfire. (Both, courtesy of Milligan College Archives.)

THE APPALACHIAN TRAIL. The Appalachian Trail, which stretches for 2,200 miles from Georgia to Maine, crosses Roan Mountain's crest. Fred Behrend (right) greets a thru-hiker in this undated photograph. The first thru-hiker to pass over the Roan was in 1936, when the trail was completed. There are several shelters on the mountain, including the Roan High Knob, the site of the former fire warden's cabin. (Courtesy of Linda Behrend.)

PICNIC ON THE ROAN. This group of unidentified residents picnic on the Roan near the Rhododendron Gardens. Since the 1950s, the National Forest Service has placed picnic tables at locations across the mountain. Prior to the tables, visitors would lay blankets on the ground for a snack or a meal. (Courtesy of Linda Behrend.)

THE RHODODENDRON FESTIVAL. Thousands of people have visited the Roan to enjoy the Rhododendron Festival. The first festival was held in 1947, and it was followed a year later by the first Rhododendron Pageant, when Betty Peoples was crowned the queen. Likely the nation's highest-altitude festival, the pageant, seen here in 1959, began as a joint effort of Roan Mountain and Bakersville civic organizations. (Courtesy of Jeannie Pippin Grizzard.)

THE BEAUTY PAGEANT. With a spectacular natural backdrop, the Roan was the Rhododendron Festival's home for decades. In this 1960 photograph, a line of pageant contestants dressed in their white gowns stroll across a field. Over the years, the pageant introduced new formats and added contests for different age groups. (Courtesy of Linda Behrend.)

THOUSANDS VISIT THE ROAN. Hundreds of people rest on the side of a hill to watch the Rhododendron Pageant. The pageant became one of the signature events in the region, attracting contestants and spectators from around the country. Some pageant winners went on to compete in the Miss America pageant. (Courtesy of Linda Perry Buchanan.)

YOUNG PAGEANT CONTESTANT. A young pageant contestant is escorted through the crowd in this 1960 Rhododendron Festival photograph. Thousands of spectators attended the event. After the festival was taken off the mountain, interest in the pageant decreased. Eventually, the pageant was discontinued, although the festival continues at Roan Mountain State Park. (Courtesy of Linda Behrend.)

RHODODENDRON FESTIVAL ENTERTAINMENT. Many entertainers take part in Rhododendron Festival activities. With their white tops and black pants, square dancers take the stage in this 1960 photograph, taken by Fred Behrend. Musicians, including local high school bands, regularly performed. Visiting queens and outgoing queens also entertained the crowds. Clogging, another festival event, is a popular Roan Mountain and Appalachian region tradition. (Courtesy of Linda Behrend.)

THE TALENT CONTEST. A pageant contestant twirls a baton during the talent portion of the Rhododendron Pageant on Roan Mountain in 1960. There were also swimsuit, evening gown, and interview portions of the pageant, which was held over a two-day period along with other festivities. (Courtesy of Linda Behrend.)

NIXON ON THE ROAN. Thousands of people attended the 1958 Rhododendron Festival to see Vice Pres. Richard Nixon. One newspaper estimated that nearly 100,000 people attended the festival. In this photograph, Roan Mountain resident Jonnie Graybeal, the wife of businessman Kenneth Wayne Graybeal, serves green beans to Nixon and his wife, Pat, on top of the mountain. The ladies of the Roan Mountain Garden Club cooked and served the couple's meal in a tent. Nixon also spoke to the crowd from a large, patriotically decorated stage. Prior to reaching Roan Mountain, Nixon's entourage participated in a large Elizabethton parade. Pat Nixon wrote a note on the back of this photograph, saying, "Thanks neighbor for the hospitality." Although Mrs. Nixon did not eat because she was ill, she said she enjoyed watching the Garden Club ladies. (Courtesy of the Graybeal family.)

WEDDING ON THE ROAN. The first couple to marry during the Rhododendron Festival was Marie Forbes, of Linville, North Carolina, and Max Potter, of Shell Creek, Tennessee, on June 21, 1953. A committee selected the couple to be the first to wed on the Roan because one was from North Carolina and the other was from Tennessee. The altar was placed on the state line. Another cross-state couple, Edith Cunningham, of Maryville, Tennessee, and Thomas Woods, of Lauren, South Carolina, married on June 20, 1954. On June 18, 1955, Tennessee governor Frank G. Clement is seen here at the wedding of Bobby McCurry, of Newland, North Carolina, and Barbara Heaton, of Roan Mountain. Another couple wed in 1956, and three couples wed in 1957. Weddings were also held in 1958, 1959, 1960, and 1961, the last year a couple was married during the Rhododendron Festival. (Courtesy of Tennessee State Library and Archives.)

PARKING ON THE ROAN. After the state widened the road to the Roan in the 1950s, thousands of visitors began attending the Rhododendron Festival. The Roan Mountain Citizens Club set up several parking areas for visitors. The parking lot seen here is filled to capacity. (Courtesy of Tennessee State Library and Archives.)

SHERMAN PIPPIN VISITS THE ROAN. East Tennessee & Western North Carolina Railroad engineer Sherman Pippin enjoyed spending time on the Roan. Pippin owned a dump truck, which he covered with a tarp and used to camp. He liked taking family members, including his niece Joanna Ledford, seen here, up the mountain to camp. (Courtesy of Joanna Ledford Miller.)

RHODODENDRON PARKING. By the 1960s, three large parking areas were established for automobiles at the annual Rhododendron Festival on the Roan. Seen here is the lot at the entrance to the Rhododendron Gardens. Later, the grounds became accessible for buses and recreational vehicles. (Courtesy of the Floyd Hayes collection.)

THE BIRD MAN. Fred Behrend (right) and Arthur Stupka, the Great Smoky Mountains National Park's first naturalist, rest on the Roan in this iconic photograph. Behrend, a German immigrant, came to Tennessee to work in Elizabethton. Known locally as the "Bird Man," he enjoyed exploring the Roan, comparing it to Germany's Black Forest. In 1959, Behrend organized the first Carter County Wildflower Tour and Bird Walk, a predecessor of the Naturalists' Rally. (Courtesy of Linda Behrend.)

BEAR WALLOW TRAIL. Following his death in 1976, Fred Behrend was honored by the Tennessee General Assembly, which dedicated Bear Wallow Trail in Roan Mountain State Park to his memory. A plaque at the trailhead reads, "Fred W. Behrend (1896–1976) — Naturalist and Lover of Roan Mountain." Several family members and friends participated in the dedication ceremony. (Courtesy of Linda Behrend.)

THE OTHER SIDE OF THE ROAN. The sparsely populated North Carolina side of Roan Mountain provides unobstructed views of the highlands. The tiny communities of Glen Ayre, Fork Mountain, and Buladean sit on the slopes of the Roan in North Carolina, and Bakersville, the seat of Mitchell County, is nearby. Mitchell County's slogan is "The Gateway to the Roan." (Courtesy of Linda Behrend.)

CARVERS GAP. Tennessee State Highway 143 and North Carolina State Highway 261 meet at Carvers Gap along the state line. The gap is the lowest point along Roan Mountain's ridgeline, and it was therefore selected to be the point where the paved highway crossed over the mountain, giving thousands of visitors access to mountaintop attractions. Both mountain approach roads opened in 1952. (Courtesy of Johnny Blankenship.)

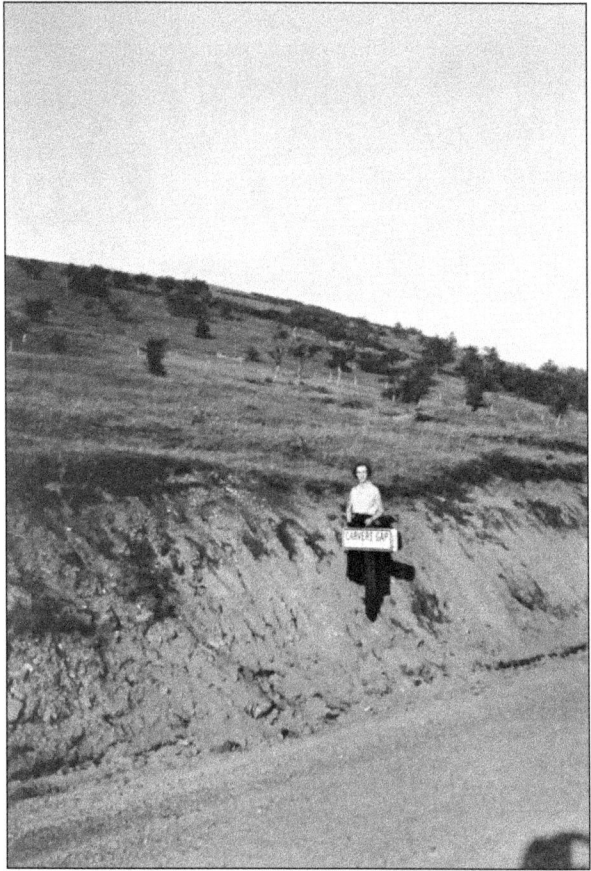

A MOUNTAIN HIGHWAY. The state highway between Burbank and Carvers Gap is a curvy two-lane road originally constructed in the early 1950s. The roadway passes through the Cherokee National Forest, where several overlooks and picnic areas have been erected for travelers. The paved road follows the general route of the old hack line road, which was a very rough dirt pathway for horses and wagons. (Courtesy of Linda Behrend.)

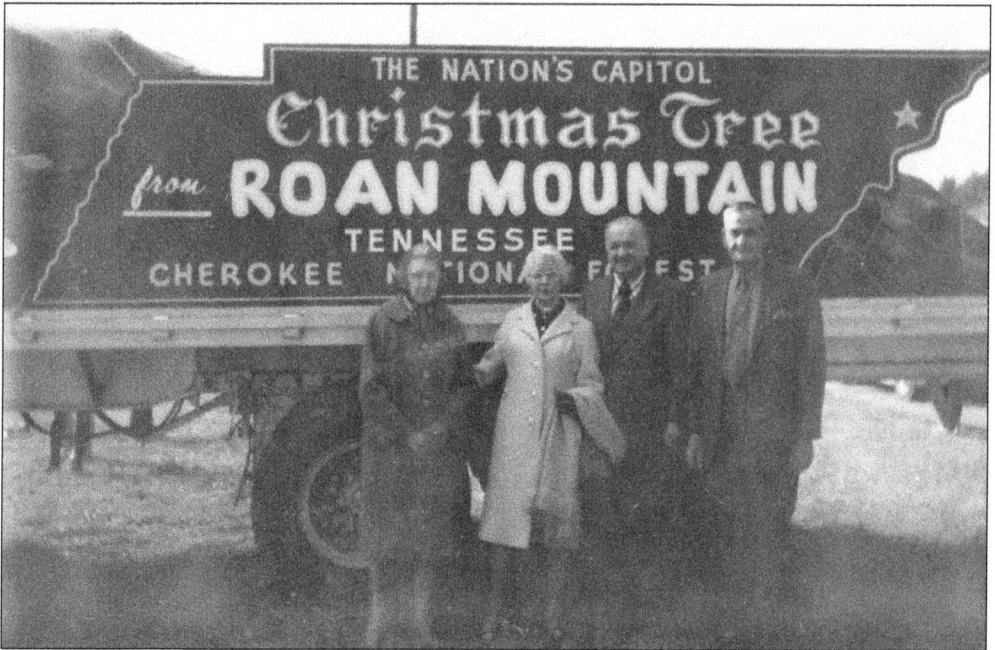

CAPITOL CHRISTMAS TREE. A large Roan Mountain fir tree was placed at the US Capitol for Christmas 1972. Newspaper articles report that a helicopter was used to lift the 50-foot Fraser fir off the snow-covered Roan. Scores of residents watched as the helicopter picked up the 3,000-pound tree. After traveling 12 miles by air, it was taken the rest of the way by tractor-trailer. (Courtesy of Jo Buchanan.)

INFLUENTIAL FAMILIES. Over the last century, many Roan Mountain families have helped secure funding for the new road to the Roan, developed and organized the Rhododendron Festival, and gained support for the creation of Roan Mountain State Park. Influential families such as the Perrys, seen here, have worked to make the mountain more accessible for visitors. (Courtesy of Linda Perry Buchanan.)

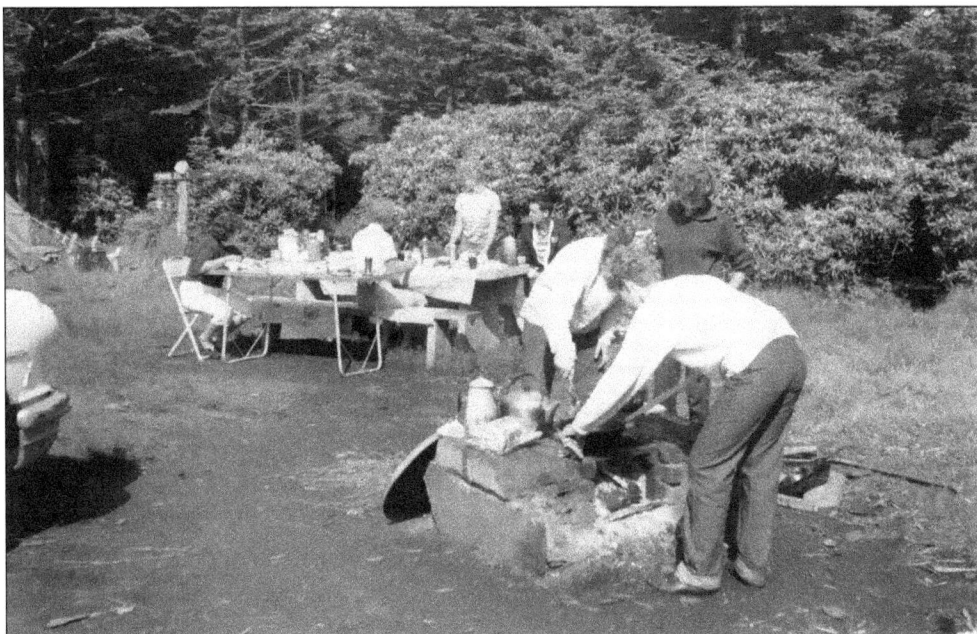

PICNICS ON THE ROAN. The beautiful Rhododendron Gardens provide the perfect backdrop for any activity. This photograph taken in the early 1960s shows a typical day for families on the Roan. Three people can be seen cooking on the outdoor grill while others rest at the table and enjoy a picnic. A tent is in the left background. (Courtesy of Durward Julian and family.)

BEHREND'S BALD. This beautiful photograph of Roan Mountain was taken in the 1940s or 1950s by Fred Behrend. The Roan's magnificent balds, scenic ridgeline, and thick forests can all be seen in this image. Behrend enjoyed photographing the mountain and its unique natural wonders. With his camera in hand, he would spend hours hiking the trails. Although he was a newspaper editor professionally, he was also an amateur photographer and bird watcher. He would capture the mountain on warm, sunny days and cold, snowy days. No matter the situation, the Roan's beauty impressed Behrend. He took many photographs of the balds, sometimes in an attempt to capture the sight of a unique bird. The "Bird Man," as he was affectionately called, found solace on the Roan. Many of his photographs, including this image, were entered in local, regional, and national contests. (Courtesy of Linda Behrend.)

DR. BROWN'S CHIMNEY. A lonely chimney stands along the Appalachian Trail on Roan Mountain in this timeless photograph. The brick chimney sitting on the side of the trail is a mystery for hikers passing over the Roan. According to Jennifer Bauer, a former Roan Mountain State Park ranger, the chimney was likely part of Dr. Dalton Milford Brown's cabin. Brown was a biology professor at East Tennessee State College in Johnson City who studied the Roan's trees. He came to the Roan as the lumber industry was destroying its forests. Brown is noted for planting a grove of fir trees on Round Bald to study their growth. The trees still stand today. In the mid-1930s, Brown spent days on the Roan, bringing along students to study. A local lumber outfit constructed the professor a cabin with a chimney. The cabin likely rotted away, but the chimney remained. It is located about halfway between the Roan High Knob Shelter and the former Cloudland Hotel site on the Appalachian Trail. (Author's collection.)

Two

ROAN MOUNTAIN VILLAGE

IN THE VILLAGE. A family poses on the lawn of the old Roan Mountain Inn for a portrait in the 1920s. The inn, located along the Doe River, is on the right. Other landmarks include the Roan Mountain depot, behind the trees, and Pierce Julian's store and house, along present-day US Highway 19E. (Courtesy of Pam Watson Braswell.)

WELCOME TO ROAN MOUNTAIN. Jane Hughes Johnson points to the old Roan Mountain sign in the 1920s. The sign included the advertisement, "A Good Place to Eat: Moreland's Café," which refers to a diner owned and operated by Hugh Moreland and his wife, Alice. The couple, who had two daughters, Lily and Ethel, operated their café next to the old iron bridge along Main Street. (Courtesy of Pam Watson Braswell.)

ROY TONCRAY IN THE VILLAGE. Roy Toncray, the son of Jackson Toncray and Sudie Pippin Toncray, who was about three years old, stands on a barrel in the village in this c. 1923 photograph. Several businesses, including a pharmacy, a general store, and an inn, anchored old Main Street. Roy died young at the age of 19. (Courtesy of Jeannie Pippin Grizzard.)

JOHN WILDER HOUSE. Union general John Wilder built an Italianate-style residence in Roan Mountain in 1884. The L-shaped home, covered in weatherboard, has had few alterations over the years. Wilder, who developed two Roan Mountain hotels, had moved from Roan Mountain to Johnson City by 1890. In the 1900s, the prominent Graybeal family purchased the property, which includes a smokehouse and a privy. (Courtesy of the National Register of Historic Places.)

GEN. JOHN WILDER. Gen. John Wilder may have not been born in Roan Mountain, but he is one of the community's most recognized and beloved residents. A Union officer during the Civil War, he discovered the Roan in the 1870s. Wilder built two resort hotels and several residences and also assisted in the development of the railroad, area mines, and other industries. (Courtesy of the Cy Crumley collection.)

The Tweetsie. The East Tennessee & Western North Carolina Railroad, or "Tweetsie," went through town from the late 1800s through the mid-1900s. It was built to transport materials from the Cranberry Mine in Western North Carolina to Johnson City. It made several stops along the route, including in Roan Mountain village, where a stationary train is captured in this photograph. (Courtesy of the Cy Crumley collection.)

Sherman Pippin. Roan Mountain native Sherman Pippin, a hack line driver and railroad engineer, was born in 1883. He is remembered as a thrifty person who would help anyone. When the railroad reached Roan Mountain, Pippin was hired to take visitors on the hack line up to the Cloudland Hotel. He later became a train engineer, a job he held for more than 50 years. (Courtesy of the Cy Crumley collection.)

ROAN MOUNTAIN INN. Gen. John Wilder constructed the Roan Mountain Inn in 1884, along the Doe River near the train station. Visitors would exit the train and stay at the inn for a few days before traveling up the mountain to the Cloudland Hotel. The three-story inn featured large guest rooms, a dining room, a lobby, a parlor, and a veranda, seen here. (Courtesy of Durward Julian and family.)

IN FRONT OF THE INN. In this 1920s photograph, from left to right, Sara Aiken Pritchard, Jane Hughes Johnson, and Florence Roark Hayes stand in front of the Roan Mountain Inn. By the mid-1900s, businessmen had torn the hotel down and built a store. Cloudland Market is located at the site of the old hotel. (Courtesy of Pam Watson Braswell.)

STAPLES FAMILY. The Staples family owned and operated the old Roan Mountain Inn in the village for several decades. Della Staples, seen at left on the inn's veranda, occasionally worked the front desk, greeting and checking in guests. Although Della and her husband, R.C. Staples, were not Roan Mountain natives, they owned a home near Cloudland High School. Their children Clara and John Staples assisted with the hotel's operations. Elmer Wolfe (below) was Staples's son from another marriage. A World War I soldier, he is seen here in front of the inn. (Both courtesy of Pam Watson Braswell.)

FIRST BAPTIST CHURCH. The First Baptist Church of Roan Mountain was established in 1889. Its first sermon was held by the Rev. David Kitzmiller. The original building was a frame structure. By 1954, a new, larger brick building was constructed. A fellowship hall and a pastorium were later built. (Courtesy of Helen Hampton.)

THE STEEL BRIDGE. Jane Hughes Johnson stands on the bank of the Doe River in Roan Mountain. The old steel bridge crosses the river behind her. The bridge has since been replaced with a concrete bridge on Main Street in the village. (Courtesy of Pam Watson Braswell.)

DRUGSTORE. Roan Mountain resident Mable Freeman stands in front of the S.B. Wood Drug Store, built in 1898 by Dr. Wood. The store always carried a full line of drugs and had an ice cream parlor for a period of time. Park Hayes assisted Dr. Wood. In 1925, Hayes's brother Fred purchased the building and renamed it Palace Drug Company. Fred Hayes retired in 1970. (Courtesy of Dillard Street.)

FRED HAYES. E. Fred Hayes owned the former Palace Drug Store for 47 years. Pictured here in the 1920s on a horse, he also participated in the Roan Mountain Citizens Club and attended First Baptist Church of Roan Mountain. He married Florence Hayes and purchased the pharmacy from S.B. Wood, who constructed the building in 1898. It is the oldest pharmacy in Tennessee. (Courtesy of Jeannie Pippin Grizzard.)

SHERMAN PIPPIN HOUSE.
Tweetsie Railroad engineer
Sherman Pippin owned a
beautiful home in Roan
Mountain along present-day
US Highway 19E. The railroad
legend and former hack line
driver purchased the farm
property in 1912. It featured a
small outbuilding at the rear
where Pippin liked to work.
At one time, the home had a
manicured lawn, trees, and a
small pond, seen at right. When
Pippin owned the house, he
allowed his extended family to
live on the property. The home,
more recently known by local
residents as the Pink House,
was eventually sold. (Both
courtesy of Joanna Miller.)

THE PIPPIN FAMILY. Several members of the Pippin family are seen here at Sherman Pippin's house. From left to right, they are identified as Earl Pippin, Frank Pippin, Hayes Pippin, Daisy Pippin Snyder, Howard Pippin, Eleanor Pippin Hertzog, Jack Pippin, and Dwayne Pippin. Sherman Pippin, who died in 1978, is buried at Johnson Cemetery, where his headstone reads, "He was a legend, loved by all." (Courtesy of Joanna Miller.)

FRANK PIPPIN HOUSE. The home of Frank and Ocha "Oakie" Hayes Pippin is seen here not long after the flood of May 1901. From left to right, Oakie (holding a baby), young Earl (lower, in the gown), Frank, Howard, and an unidentified Pippin child pose for a photograph on the porch. The home, built about 1900, still stands today behind the pharmacy in Roan Mountain. (Courtesy of Jeannie Pippin Grizzard.)

THE SLAUGHTER FAMILY. The Slaughter family is one of Roan Mountain's most influential families, having developed several properties in the community, including the movie theater, stores, garages, and homes. Robert "Bob" Odell Slaughter, his wife, Myrtle Evelin Julian Slaughter, and their daughter Geraldine Peggy Slaughter are seen at right in a 1944 family portrait. The Slaughters first lived along Main Street, but later built a beautiful river rock home on State Highway 143 near Magill Memorial Presbyterian Church, where they regularly held social events. The couple also participated in the local citizens club. Bob Slaughter is seen below in the 1920s, apparently seeking a female acquaintance. (Both courtesy of Bill Whitehead.)

THE ROAN THEATRE. Bob Slaughter built the Roan Theatre, a traditional movie house, along Main Street in Roan Mountain in 1948. The theater was part of a stretch of businesses known as the Slaughter block. The Freeman family operated the theater with the help of the Slaughters. For many years, Myrtle Slaughter was the only person to sell tickets. Others operated the projector, the popcorn machine, and other aspects of the theater. The Slaughters' daughter Geraldine said the first movie she saw at the theater was *Slave Girl*, which came out in 1947. Students from nearby Cloudland High School regularly visited the theater to see movies such as *Ben-Hur*. After the high school burned down in 1957, graduation ceremonies were held at the theater in 1958 and 1959. The theater eventually closed in the 1970s. A church most recently occupied the building. (Courtesy of Tennessee State Library and Archives.)

BURLESON & SON SUPER MARKET. The Burleson & Son Super Market was built by Bob Slaughter in the 1940s. By 1957 future state senator Robert "Bob" Burleson had bought the grocery section, and Harry Heaton had bought the hardware section. When Heaton's store moved to a different location a year later, Burleson expanded his store into the vacated section. Burleson later purchased the Roanview Dairyland, changing the name to Bob's Dairyland. (Courtesy of Tennessee State Library and Archives.)

THE ROAN CAFÉ. The Roan Café was located next to the Roan Theatre along Main Street in Roan Mountain. Virginia Burleson ran the small luncheonette until she moved her restaurant business to the café next to the motel on old State Highway 143. From left to right, Elisha Garland Jr., Georgia Triplett, and Betty Garland are seen at the café. The cafe had signs that read, "Steak; Chicken; Chops; Sandwiches." (Courtesy of Jeannie Perkins.)

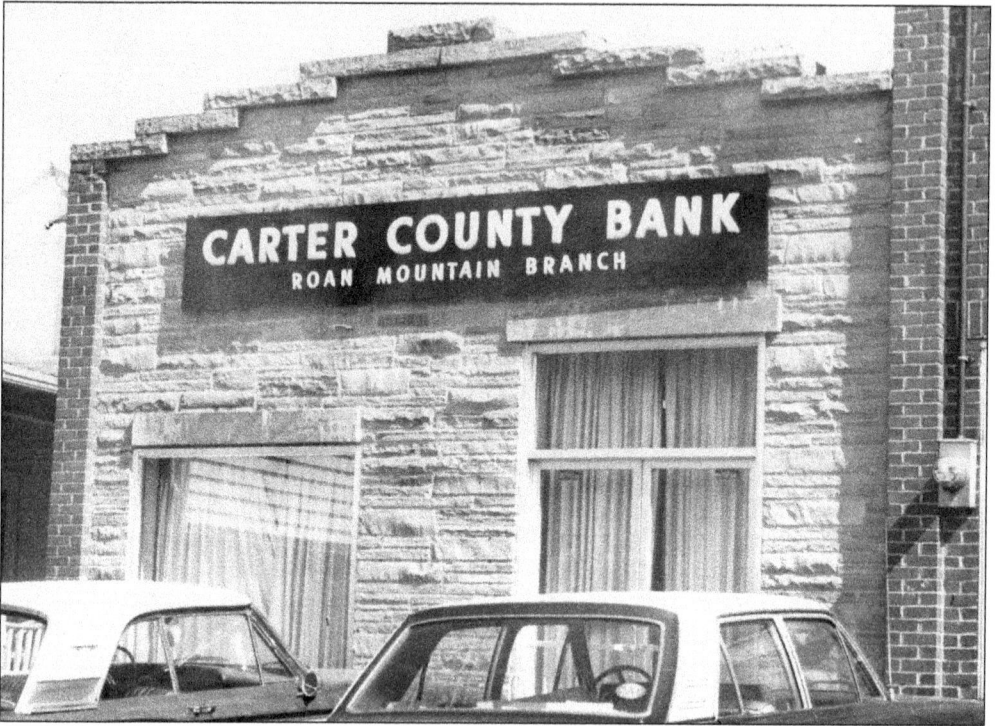

Carter County Bank. The first Carter County Bank branch in Roan Mountain, seen above, opened in 1950. Community members had sought a bank branch in Roan Mountain for years and finally received interest from Carter County Bank in Elizabethton. Local businessman Bob Slaughter constructed the bank building next to the movie theater along Main Street. It had two employees. Bill Whitehead, Slaughter's grandson, said bank robbers broke into the theater and dug through a wall in an attempt to reach the bank vault. When they hit metal, the robbers gave up and left. In 1973, the branch moved to the building seen below on US Highway 19E. The bank is now housed in a new building. (Both courtesy of Carter County Bank.)

HERB AND ROOTS WAREHOUSE. After the East Tennessee & Western North Carolina Railroad came to Roan Mountain, the influential Graybeal family built a warehouse in the village. The C.R. Graybeal & Sons warehouse stored roots and herbs for medicinal use. It was believed to be the largest roots and herb warehouse in the country. Above, two mountaineers, Jesse Hardin (left) and Ed Calhoun (second from left), bring sacks of herbs to the warehouse. The photograph below shows Byron F. Graybeal (left) and Andrew Hardin with sacks of roots and herbs in 1940. The Graybeal family also owned a pipe stem factory and a flooring facility in the village. (Both courtesy of Tennessee State Library and Archives.)

PIPE FACTORY. Two men saw rhododendron burl roots for pipe stems at one of the Graybeal family's facilities in Roan Mountain in 1941. When materials from Europe became scarce during wars, manufacturers sought Appalachian rhododendron, including the famed groves on Roan Mountain. Other such facilities were established in the mountains of North Carolina. (Courtesy of Tennessee State Library and Archives.)

THE GRAYBEAL FAMILY. Roan Mountain business leader Cicero R. Graybeal and his wife, Florence Calhoun Graybeal, pose with three of their children, from left to right, Kenneth Wayne Graybeal, Alice Graybeal, and Byron F. Graybeal. Their second daughter, Margaret Graybeal, was born in 1914, a year after this photograph was taken. The Graybeal family owned several homes in Roan Mountain, including the John Wilder Home. (Courtesy of the Graybeal family.)

GRAYBEALS AT THE WAREHOUSE. Byron Graybeal (left) and his father, C.R. Graybeal, are pictured beside the herb and roots warehouse in Roan Mountain. The shadow of Kenneth Wayne Graybeal, who is taking the photograph, is visible. The Graybeal family operated several large warehouses and manufacturing businesses in Roan Mountain and in other cities around the country. The company had its headquarters in the village. (Courtesy of the Graybeal family.)

BYRON GRAYBEAL'S HOME. The elder C.R. Graybeal is pictured between his two sons, Byron F. Graybeal (left) and Kenneth Wayne Graybeal. The photograph was taken outside of Byron Graybeal's brick home. The family business, C.R. Graybeal & Sons, was at one time the largest buyer of crude botanical drugs in the United States. The business also ventured into prefabricated homes and nuclear technology. (Courtesy of the Graybeal family.)

ROAN MOUNTAIN YOUTH. Over the decades, Roan Mountain youth have had several venues for entertainment. They could go visit the Dairyland for burgers and shakes or the Tea Room for a round of billiards. At the back of the old fire hall on Main Street, volunteers set up a skating rink. This group of students attended Cloudland High School and was photographed in the village. (Courtesy of Linda Perry Buchanan.)

HOMECOMING PARADE. The Cloudland High School homecoming parade is a tradition in Roan Mountain. Hundreds of local residents line the streets to watch the passing cars and floats. Dede McKinney is seen here resting on the hood of a car on Main Street. She is passing the old Goodson House, one of several homes built by John Wilder. (Courtesy of the Cloudland High School annual.)

ROAN MOUNTAIN UNITED METHODIST CHURCH. The first church organized in Roan Mountain was the Methodist Episcopal church. In 1885, Gen. John Wilder donated land for the building. The first trustees were Wilder, Henderson Folsom, E.E. Hunter, L.H. Rhudy, W.P. Dungan, B.F. Folsom, and W. Boling. The church was originally a one-room building. (Courtesy of Pam Watson Braswell.)

TRAVELING PASTORS. The Roan Mountain United Methodist Church congregation is seen here on Easter Sunday in 1957. Very few of the early church pastors lived in Roan Mountain. They would take the train on Saturday, spend the weekend in the village, and return home by train on Monday. The Rev. Dawson Rowe (1876–1910) lived in a nearby home. (Courtesy of Pam Watson Braswell.)

MAGILL MEMORIAL CHURCH. Magill Memorial Presbyterian Church was built in stages in the 1940s on State Highway 143 in Roan Mountain. The organization of the church began in 1938 at lifelong member Pearl Brown's home. Brown is noted as having perfect attendance at Magill. The photograph at left shows, from left to right, Larry, Thelma, and Ronnie Julian and the family dog, named Kitty, in front of the church shortly after it was constructed. At the time, the road from the village to the Roan was made of dirt and gravel. The photograph below, taken in 1945, shows, from left to right, Ronnie Julian, Lanny Julian (in front), unidentified, Johnny Forbes, Jim Burleson, unidentified, Tom Burleson (in front), two unidentified girls, and Larry Julian standing in front of Magill. The Sunday school teacher is Thelma Julian. (Both courtesy of Durward Julian and family.)

ROAN MOUNTAIN VOLUNTEER FIRE DEPARTMENT. In the early 1960s, a concerned group of men organized the Roan Mountain Volunteer Fire Department. Finley Miller and Durward Julian were named the first captains. The department purchased a GMC truck with a front mount pump. Water was pumped from streams. At first the group raised funds by selling fruitcakes, but when the need came to build a fire hall, they began holding wrestling events and music concerts. The department is training in these 1960s photographs. The image above shows, from left to right, (first row) Johnson City captain Clarence Eades, Emmett Greene, Bobby McCurry, Eddie Burleson, and Roan Mountain captain Finley Miller, pointing at the hoses; (second row) Ford Miller, Lee Stout, Perry Markland, John G. Markland, unidentified, Zeb McCloud, R.L. Miller, unidentified, Jimmy Dean Arnett, and Larry Dean Markland. (Both courtesy of Karen Markland Julian.)

NATURALISTS' RALLY AT MOTEL. Local businessman Zeb McCloud and his wife, Tharon, built the one-story Roan Mountain Motel in the 1950s. After McCloud became the first Roan Mountain State Park superintendent, he sold the motel to his sister Hazel McCloud. The Roan Mountain Naturalists' Rally, seen here, later met at the motel. Elvis Presley is rumored to have stayed at the motel while visiting Roan Mountain. (Courtesy of Linda Behrend.)

GRILL AND MOTEL. The A & J Motel operated between 1957 and 1970 on old State Highway 143. It was named after Adrian Julian and James Julian Jr. The Roan Grill was adjacent to the motel. Three young men, including John Orr in the middle, are seen here standing outside the old Roan Grill. Orr said friends regularly went to the grill. (Courtesy of John and Phyllis Orr.)

THE ROANVIEW DAIRYLAND. For decades, Roan Mountain residents, young and old, have gathered at the Dairyland on US Highway 19E for burgers and shakes. Lige Hampton built the Roanview Dairyland in the 1950s. With two walk-up windows, it became a popular hangout for local youth. Bob Burleson bought the diner in the early 1960s and changed the name to Bob's Dairyland. (Courtesy of Bob's Dairyland.)

ROY TROUTMAN'S STATION. Roy Troutman Sr., the son of Hezekiah Troutman of Burbank, owned and operated a service station in Roan Mountain village for several decades. It was located along US Highway 19E. In this photograph, Pierce Julian's store and the S.B. Wood Drug Store are visible. Only the drugstore remains open. (Courtesy of Floyd Odom.)

CLOUDLAND HIGH SCHOOL. Cloudland High School was built in Roan Mountain in 1928. It was a modern and well-equipped school. Tragedy struck in 1957 when a fire destroyed the school. The county later voted to construct the present building near the site of the original. The school is seen here in March 1945 during a snowstorm. (Courtesy of John and Phyllis Orr.)

HIGHLANDER FOOTBALL. The first Cloudland High School 11-man football team is seen here in 1950. The team included, from left to right, (first row) Ray Taylor, Pete Buck, Bob Crain, Harry Morgan, Carliss Powell, John Heifner, and Bill Brown; (second row) Bob Burleson, Bill Hughes, John Orr, and Sonny Ellis. (Courtesy of John and Phyllis Orr.)

CLASS OF 1939. Many class pictures were taken on the Cloudland High School steps, including this one from 1939. From left to right are (first row) Florence Julian, Geraldine McKinney, Arlys Biggs, and Florine Julian; (second row) Helen Stout, Edith Johnson, Paul Hopson, Blake Ellis, Julia Keys, and Ham Ray; (third row) Frankie Winters, Corinth Heaton, Lucy Johnson, and Goldia Blackwell; (fourth row) Marion Johnson, Christine Keller, Lillie Mae Cordell, Oledia Julian, and Jessie Berry; (fifth row) Pauline Heaton. (Courtesy of Martha Whaley.)

SONNY SMITH. Roan Mountain native Sonny Smith was a head basketball coach for 22 seasons at several major universities. He helped turn around losing programs at East Tennessee State University and Auburn University. He also coached at Virginia Commonwealth University. Here, young Sonny Smith (left) and his brother Jim sit on the lap of their mother, Irma Smith. Their father, Grigg Smith, is not pictured. (Courtesy of the Smith family.)

AUSTIN JULIAN JR. Future Air Force lieutenant colonel Austin Julian Jr. is seen here in a basketball uniform outside the high school. Born in 1922 to Betty Ellen and Austin Julian, he was the youngest of 10 children. During his 29 years as a test pilot, he flew more than 85,000 miles in 118 different aircraft. One mission brought him flying over Roan Mountain. (Courtesy of Martha Whaley.)

HIGH SCHOOL FIRE. Tragedy struck Roan Mountain in 1957 when fire destroyed Cloudland High School. Beginning above a first-floor restroom, the fire spread quickly through the occupied building. Everyone escaped, but the school was lost. Students returned after Christmas break and attended classes at the high school's agriculture building, the Holiness Church, and Cloudland Elementary School. Graduation was held at the Roan Theatre. (Courtesy of Cloudland High School.)

RICHARD WINTERS. Roan Mountain native Richard Winters has worn many hats over the years. He was the principal of Cloudland High School in this photograph, taken in the 1970s. A Marine veteran who graduated from the school two years after the 1957 school fire, Winters served for many years as the principal before serving as a Carter County commissioner and on the school board. (Courtesy of Cloudland High School.)

DOE RIVER FLOODS. In the 20th century, Roan Mountain was struck by two major flooding events, one in 1901 and one in 1998. Following the 1998 flood, Vice Pres. Al Gore met with residents at Cloudland Elementary School. Large portions of the village were underwater during both floods, when deluges of rainfall sent the Doe River gushing over its banks. The impact was devastating. (Courtesy of Jo Buchanan.)

THE ORR HOME. Brownlow Orr was an influential Roan Mountain farmer, store operator, and early postmaster. He and his wife, Myra Ramsey Orr, built this large home in the village near Cloudland High School. They had four children, three of whom lived to adulthood: Robert, Annie, and Edith. Robert and his wife, Cordelia, had five children: Ruth Ann, Bill, Jessica, Mary, and John. (Courtesy of John and Phyllis Orr.)

MILKING THE COW. Cordelia Orr milks a cow on her family's farm in Roan Mountain. She did much of the farm work, as her husband, Robert "Bob" Orr, worked for the county road department and Elizabethton rayon plants. In 1958, a portion of the farm was sold to the county to rebuild Cloudland High School following the fire of 1957. (Courtesy of John and Phyllis Orr.)

TOM GRAY. Roan Mountain enthusiast Tom Gray, affectionately called the "Rugged Dreamer," is seen here in a photograph taken by Fred Behrend. Gray was influential in developing Roan Mountain State Park, the Sycamore Shoals State Historic Area, the Overmountain Victory Trail, the Roan Mountain Naturalists' Rally, and local botany programs. A monument was erected in his honor at the entrance to the Roan Mountain State Park visitors' center. (Courtesy of Linda Behrend.)

4-H CHAMPIONS. Four Roan Mountain students went to Nashville in 1983 to accept an award for being Tennessee's 4-H state forestry judging champions. Seen here from left to right are (first row) State Rep. Bob Percy, State Sen. Bob Burleson of Roan Mountain, and State Rep. Zane Whitson; (second row) Tony Presnell, Rodney Stocton, Chris Street, Anthony Roberts, and Keith Hart. (Courtesy of Keith Hart.)

DALE AND RUTH PERRY. Dale Perry taught school for 42 years as a vocational principal and a teacher at Cloudland High School and Happy Valley High School. He was instrumental in the development of Roan Mountain State Park and creating road access to the Roan. He and his wife, Lillian Ruth Perry, were members of Gray's Chapel Presbyterian Church. They had two daughters, Linda and Judy. (Courtesy of Linda Perry Buchanan.)

JAMES POTTER. James Potter and his wife, Edna Potter, were influential members of the Roan Mountain community. He was the principal of Cloudland High School and a charter member of the Roan Mountain Citizens Club. A Navy veteran who served in World War II, he was also instrumental in starting the Naturalists' Rally. (Courtesy of Edna Potter.)

AT THE SLAUGHTER HOME. Judge James N. Julian (left) and Sen. Albert Gore Sr. chat at Bob Slaughter's home in Roan Mountain. Slaughter is seen behind and in between the two men. Tennessee governor Gordon Browning also visited the home to discuss the new road to be built up the Roan. (Courtesy of Durward Julian and family.)

SANDERS YOUNG. Seen here at his property near the drugstore, Sanders Young was a successful Roan Mountain merchant in the early 1900s. Young and his wife, Sallie Little Young, established their home in Roan Mountain. In addition to retail, Sanders owned a hack line that drove visitors to the top of Roan Mountain. He also was the postmaster in 1908. (Courtesy of Patsy Young Crum.)

ROAN MOUNTAIN GARDEN CLUB. The 1961–1962 officers of the Roan Mountain Garden Club gathered at the Rhododendron Gift Shop in the village for this photograph. The club included, from left to right, Ruth Graybeal, Willie Cates, Grace Tomlinson, Mary Alice Hampton, Ruby Ford, Rhett Greer, Clara Allen, and Patricia Aldridge. Many influential women in Roan Mountain were active in the garden club. (Courtesy of Jackie and Dawn Peters.)

JULIAN FAMILY REUNION. About 600 people attended the 1947 Julian family reunion held at Judge James N. Julian's property in Roan Mountain. In this photograph, members of the "House of Julian," as a newspaper called them, gathered at the judge's house, located near the Shelving Rock. Julian stood in the back of a truck and recited the family's history as guests enjoyed activities and food. (Courtesy of Durward Julian and family.)

THE GREER FAMILY.
Ray Greer, an active
Roan Mountain
resident, is seen
here with family
and friends. Greer
taught and coached
at Cloudland High
School and was also
a manager at Carter
County Bank's Roan
Mountain branch.
In addition, he
and his wife, Rhett
Greer, participated
in the Roan
Mountain Citizens
Club and the Roan
Mountain Garden
Club. (Courtesy of
Linda Behrend.)

WINTER 1936. The Roan Mountain community experienced a wild year of weather in 1936, as the rest of the country had blizzards, droughts, record-breaking heat, and flooding. Roan Mountain was buried under several feet of snow following a paralyzing and historic storm during the winter months, seen here, and then sweated through temperatures reaching 100 degrees in the summer. (Courtesy of Pam Watson Braswell.)

DR. MURRELL PINSON. One of Roan Mountain's leading physicians in the mid-1900s, Dr. Murrell Pinson had an office near the Roan Mountain post office but also made many house calls. The doctor delivered several hundred Roan Mountain babies and was a popular family physician. In this picture with family and friends, he is the elderly gentleman sitting on the couch. (Courtesy of Pam Watson Braswell.)

JANE HUGHES JOHNSON. Jane Hughes Johnson, who married Robert "Bob" Johnson, could be spotted around the village. In this photograph, taken in the early 1930s, she is seen near Myrtle Miller's store on old US Highway 19E. The store's canopy, which was located behind the post office, can be seen in the background. A local bridge was later dedicated to Bob Johnson, a former state employee. (Courtesy of Pam Watson Braswell.)

Three

BURBANK TO HAMPTON CREEK

BURBANK SIGN. Burbank, which was settled during the Civil War, is located between Roan Mountain State Park and Carvers Gap along State Highway 143. It is named after Indiana native John A. Burbank. Here, in the 1940s, W.L. Brown and Frank Brown stand next to the old Burbank sign. The sign was located at the old Burbank Road and Cove Creek Road split. (Courtesy of Tennessee State Library and Archives.)

BURBANK STORES. Roan Mountain residents and tourists alike stopped at Harrell's Store in Burbank on their way to the Roan. The predecessor to Jack's, Harrell's Store offered an assortment of goods and services for customers. At left, Dave Harrell stands out front of his store in the mid-1940s. In addition to operating the store, Harrell and his wife, Rhoda, were influential in the community and attended Magill Memorial Presbyterian Church. Jess Troutman is seen below at his store in Burbank in the 1950s. The store, which carried an assortment of items, was open in the 1950s and 1960s. (Left, courtesy of Jo Buchanan; below, courtesy of Ruth Barnett.)

MAIL BY HORSEBACK. Even after the automobile was introduced, mailmen in rural Roan Mountain continued to deliver mail by horseback. Steven Street, born in 1865, is seen here in the 1920s taking a package to a resident in the Burbank area. Street rode daily by horseback to carry letters and packages. The young boy on the fence has been identified as J.L. Troutman. (Courtesy of Esta Street Stevens.)

DAY TRIP TO THE ROAN. Burbank's Troutman family is pictured in the 1930s on a day trip to the top of the Roan. The entire family regularly went by horse to reach the mountaintop. This photograph was part of a series of images depicting the journey. Another photograph shows two elderly Troutman family members standing in the back of the wagon, and a third shows the family posing for a portrait. (Courtesy of Ruth Barnett.)

DAVID AND ISABELLE HONEYCUTT. Early Burbank residents David and Isabelle Honeycutt pose for a photograph in the 1940s on their property in Burbank. The couple regularly traveled up the mountain to provide food, goods, and other services to guests staying at the Cloudland Hotel. The hotel operated until the 1910s. To reach the landmark hotel, the Honeycutts journeyed up the narrow, dirt hack line road. (Courtesy of Peggy Tipton Hershey.)

HONEYCUTT BROTHERS. David and Isabelle Honeycutt had five sons and a daughter. All of the children became influential Roan Mountain residents. Seen here from left to right are Paul, Frank, Zeb, and Fred Honeycutt, Lon Tipton, and Sam Honeycutt, David Honeycutt's half-brother from North Carolina. The couple's fifth son, Earl, and daughter, Mae, are not pictured in this 1959 image. Mae married Lon Tipton. (Courtesy of Peggy Tipton Hershey.)

BURBANK FREEWILL BAPTIST CHURCH. Children participating in bible school at Burbank Freewill Baptist in 1962 pose in front of the church, located at the foot of Roan Mountain. The church was first established in 1865 and had 12 charter members. It was known as Forbes Chapel in honor of David Forbes, who donated land. In 1967, the congregation built a new facility. (Courtesy of Ruth Barnett.)

SUGAR HOLLOW CHURCH. The 1940s congregation of Sugar Hollow Christian Church included, from left to right, (first row) Anna Bell Buchanan, Junior Buchanan, Louise McKinney, Dollie Sue Moore, Velma Moore, Helen McKinney, and Erma Johnson; (second row) Wilson Thomas, S.D. Thomas, General Buchanan, Dokie Buchanan, Mary Birchfield, Myrtle McKinney, and Sarah Birchfield; (third row) Clarence Johnson, Juanita Johnson, Jim Buchanan, Vadie Buchanan, and Bessie Johnson; (fourth row) Lee McKinney, Birtie Miller, Lee Birchfield, and Ralph McKinney. (Courtesy of Dillard Street.)

GRAY'S CHAPEL. Gray's Chapel is a rock Presbyterian church in the Hampton Creek community of Roan Mountain. It was established in May 1927 and is named in honor of Rev. J.L. Gray. The reverend also worked with the congregation at Magill Memorial Presbyterian. The Overmountain Men, from northeastern Tennessee and southwestern Virginia, passed near the site of the chapel on their journey to the Battle of Kings Mountain during the Revolutionary War. The congregation is seen above in the 1940s. The photograph below was taken in the late 1900s of Dale Perry retrieving the church's time capsule during a special event. Perry and his family were active members of the church. (Above, courtesy of Jo Buchanan; below, courtesy of Linda Perry Buchanan.)

UNKNOWN PHOTOGRAPH. A group of individuals, dressed in late-19th- or early-20th-century attire, stands underneath a wooden structure in this unidentified vintage photograph. Some of the men appear to be holding axes and picks. A railroad bed seems to go through the structure, and the walls are lined with machinery. It may be a mining operation or a lumber camp. (Courtesy of Linda Perry Buchanan.)

FIELD WORK. T.R. Street works in the field with his horses in the Heaton Creek area. Roan Mountain residents have worked hard over the years to care for their gardens and fields, hooking up plows and trailers to their horses, mules, oxen, and other animals on their farms. (Courtesy of Dillard Street.)

MACK TIPTON'S STORE. Ezekiel "Mack" Tipton operated a store in Hampton Creek in the 1920s and 1930s. He was disabled and had nine children, but he still managed to operate the business. Tipton's store was located next to his home, so his family constructed a ramp between the two structures. He would sit in a chair and rock his way between the two. (Courtesy of Jennifer Fleenor Sizemore.)

THE BOONE FAMILY. The Heck N. and Eugenia Julian Boone family is seen here at a 1956 reunion at their home in Hampton Creek. The Boones of Roan Mountain are direct descendants of frontiersman Daniel Boone. Boone family members have been active in the community, and many have operated stores or farmed. Crumley Boone made long rifles. (Courtesy of Jennifer Fleenor Sizemore.)

THE JARRETT FAMILY. The Willie and Myra Street Jarrett family successfully began an orchard-growing tradition in the Burbank community. The Jarretts had eight children, including McKinley and Vester Jarrett, seen here with their parents in the 1920s. The other children were Clifford, Jessie, Ervin, Mary, Paul, and Earl. While all of the children became farmers, Vester also operated a store at Smith Branch. (Courtesy of Jeannie Perkins.)

JARRETT'S ORCHARD. From left to right, Harold Jarrett, Dr. Harry Williams of the University of Tennessee Extension, Jess Jarrett, and Tom Peters, also of the UT Extension, are seen here at Jarrett's apple orchard in Burbank. The Jarrett family has long owned orchards in the community. Jess Jarrett was a member of the Apple Growers' Association and was on the board of directors of the Carter County Farm Bureau. (Courtesy of Keith Hart.)

THE STOCTON FAMILY. The Stocton family lived at the foot of Roan Mountain in the Cove Creek community. John and Julia Hughes Stocton had 10 children, and the large family had a farm. As the children grew up, they purchased land nearby and started their own farms. These family members are, from left to right, Lois, Dorothy, Marshall, Ida, Claude, Nola, Mary, Spence, John, Paul, Julia, and Edna. (Courtesy of Gary Stocton.)

COVE CREEK SCHOOL. Constructed by the Works Progress Administration, the rock schoolhouse at Cove Creek opened in 1933. The basketball team is seen here shortly after the school opened. The teams played outdoors on dirt courts at several different schools. Players either walked or rode in the back of a truck to reach games. Walter Keys was the coach. (Courtesy of the *Elizabethton Star*.)

76

THE TROUTMAN FAMILY. The Troutman family has resided along Burbank Road for more than a century. Primarily a farming family, members have also gotten into retail. Jess and Roy Troutman operated service stations and stores. Seen here from left to right are Chrissy, Willie, Hezekiah, Vista, Lisa, Dave, Nervie, Robert, Nettie, and Jess Troutman. They are arranged from oldest to youngest. (Courtesy of J.L. Troutman.)

TROUTMAN FAMILY HOME. The Troutman family homestead was built in 1935 on Burbank Road in Roan Mountain. While Floyd Greer constructed the house, the family lived in the nearby Burbank schoolhouse. The home had four bedrooms, and the basement walls were built out of rocks from the fields. Seen from left to right on the lawn are Guy, Jack, Delia, Ralph, J.L., and Willie Troutman. (Courtesy of J.L. Troutman.)

JOHN FREEMAN'S GUN. John Freeman, born in the 1870s, was a farmer who carried his gun everywhere he went. He lived in the Roan Mountain area for a short time and died in Pineola, North Carolina, at the age of 93. Many men carried firearms with them in the early 1900s. (Courtesy of Esta Street Stevens.)

THE MCCLOUD FAMILY. In 1900, W.T. McCloud and his wife, Martha Ann Hyder, bought the Crab Orchard Iron Company's house at Peg Leg Mine, which was located in what would eventually become Roan Mountain State Park. McCloud later built a large Victorian home in the village. Seen here from left to right are (first row) Zeb, W.T., Martha, Naomi, and Hazel McCloud; (second row) Bonnie, Ruth, Noland, Joe, and Dorothy McCloud. (Courtesy of Jackie and Dawn Peters.)

RURAL STREET SIGNS. Rural street signs can be found throughout the valleys, hollows, and mountains of the Roan Mountain area. The wooden signs are mounted to poles at crossroads to direct travelers trying to find their way. In the early and mid-1900s, these landmark signs became photographic subjects. Many Roan Mountain residents have old photographs of signs, such as those at Carvers Gap, Heaton Creek, Burbank, and Shell Creek. Ray Freeman and Dillard Street are seen at right at an old sign directing travelers to the Heaton Branch and Burbank communities. The photograph above shows a rural scene in Heaton Creek. (Both courtesy of Dillard Street.)

SHELVING ROCK ENCAMPMENT. During the Revolutionary War, the Overmountain Men stored gunpowder at Shelving Rock, known by locals as Sheltering Rock, located along State Highway 143 near Roan Mountain State Park. The Overmountain Men passed through Roan Mountain on their journey to Kings Mountain, South Carolina, where they defeated British troops in October 1780. The Overmountain Men originated at Sycamore Shoals in Elizabethton before venturing through Gap Creek and then Roan Mountain. They also passed through Hampton Creek before crossing the mountain into North Carolina. Mary Patton and her husband supplied gunpowder to the men, who stored it under the rock ledge. Patton and her husband operated a mill near Elizabethton. The Overmountain Men and their horses also rested in the fields near Shelving Rock. (Courtesy of Tennessee State Library and Archives.)

STATE PARK DEDICATION. Gen. William Westmoreland (center left) and local resident David Harrell (center right) chat at the dedication ceremony for the new visitors' center at Roan Mountain State Park in 1980. General Westmoreland commanded US military operations during the Vietnam War. Other officials present included US representative Jimmy Quillen and several local leaders. (Courtesy of Jo Buchanan.)

APPALACHIAN MUSIC. The Roan Mountain Hilltoppers are seen here performing at Roan Mountain State Park. Although Bill Birchfield is missing from this photograph, the other band members are, from left to right, Ethel, Creed, and Joe Birchfield. The popular old-time string band performs traditional Appalachian music. They have been performing since 1974. Other bands, such as the Roan Mountain Moonshiners, continue to play Appalachian music in the area as well. (Courtesy of Jennifer Bauer.)

THE MILL WHEEL. James W. Potter is shown around 1950 at a gristmill that was owned and operated by William S. Farmer on Trivette Branch in the Poga community. The mill was still in use when this photograph was taken in 1950. It is now a permanent fixture at the visitors' center at Roan Mountain State Park, along State Highway 143. In the 1960s, the state purchased the mill wheel for use at the state park. With the help of Frank Dyer and Carl Smith, Zeb McCloud, the park's first superintendent, disassembled the waterwheel. A truck from Warriors Path State Park in Kingsport was used to transport the wheel to Roan Mountain. McCloud, Dyer, and Smith them reassembled the mill wheel at its present site. A flume was erected from the Doe River to make the waterwheel operate. (Courtesy of Edna Potter.)

RHODODENDRON FESTIVAL AT THE PARK. After Roan Mountain State Park officially opened in the 1970s, the local citizens club held its annual Rhododendron Festival at the new visitors' center along State Highway 143. Prior to moving to the state park, the festival was held on top of the mountain near the Rhododendron Gardens. Due to the inconvenience and costs of setting up the festival on the mountain, the citizens club decided to move the annual event to the valley. Entertainers performed on a small stage at the foot of the ramp that crosses the Doe River. The area provided less space than previous festival locations. Former park ranger Jennifer Bauer said it was a "wee bit crowded." After a couple of years outside of the visitors' center, the citizens club moved the festival to its current location near the campground and conference center. Thousands of people continue to enjoy the festivities today. (Courtesy of Jennifer Bauer.)

DAVID MILLER HOMESTEAD. David Miller came to Roan Mountain in the early 1870s and built a log cabin. The home eventually rotted away, but by 1908, his son Nathaniel had built a new house. Descendants owned the property until the state purchased it in 1969. Lloyd Miller and Sally Miller Joslyn are seen here outside the home, which is now part of Roan Mountain State Park. (Courtesy of Joanna Miller.)

HOMESTEAD INTERPRETER. John Frank Miller was Roan Mountain State Park's first interpreter at the historical David Miller Homestead. Between 1983 and 1995, Miller provided guests with tours and information about the old farm, located on Strawberry Mountain off of State Highway 143. Frank, David Miller's grandson, was one of several descendants to work at the historical site; he also lived there with his father, Nathaniel Miller. (Courtesy of Jennifer Bauer.)

Four

SHELL CREEK TO
BUCK MOUNTAIN

SHELL CREEK SCHOOL. The Lower Shell Creek School, a Roan Mountain landmark, was constructed in 1911. It consisted of two floors and had a white clapboard exterior. At various times, the school housed grades one through twelve. Classes continued at Shell Creek until the 1950s, when students began attending Cloudland. This photograph appears to have been taken on Election Day. (Courtesy of Linda Brinkley Morgan.)

CHURCH HOUSE AND STORE. The beautiful Church House is located at the corner of US Highway 19E and Shell Creek Road. It was built by William Church and his wife, Lula Cornelia Hardin, in 1882. Prior to constructing the house, they lived in a smaller home on a hill behind the property. They built the house and a store in anticipation of the railroad coming through the community. The Shell Creek depot sat across from the store on the other side of the tracks. Church utilized the train for incoming merchandise. After Church died in 1889, Lula Hardin married John Snider. The train passed through Shell Creek until the 1940s, when a flood destroyed the tracks. The most recent owner, Julia Kodak, said her family located ledgers in the store building. The ledgers featured the names of several prominent local residents, including the Potters, Shells, Ellises, Woodruffs, and Harrisons. (Courtesy of Linda Brinkley Morgan.)

AT SHELL CREEK. An elderly man stands along the railroad tracks in Shell Creek in this photograph. The community is named after pioneer settlers Daniel and Polly Shell, who came to Shell Creek in the early 1800s and had 10 children. The couple is buried at the historical cemetery beside Morgan Branch Freewill Baptist Church. (Courtesy of the Cy Crumley collection.)

OLD LOWER SHELL CREEK CHURCH. Lower Shell Creek Christian Church was built on J.W. Brinkley's land in 1917. The congregation, which was first established in 1909, later built a new facility across the road on US Highway 19E. Many prominent families, including the Youngs, Brinkleys, and Churches, attended Lower Shell Creek Christian Church. (Courtesy of Linda Brinkley Morgan.)

LOWER SHELL CREEK SCHOOL. The Lower Shell Creek School had a very large student population. It was one of the largest schools in the Roan Mountain community in the early 1900s. At times, the school housed grades one through twelve. It was a predecessor of Cloudland High School. (Courtesy of Linda Brinkley Morgan.)

LAST MAIL DAY. David Ellis and Austin Thomas delivered mail for the Shell Creek post office for the last time on a snowy December day in 1955. Evelyn Brinkley Young, the postmaster, and her employees then began working at the Roan Mountain office. Pres. Franklin D. Roosevelt had appointed Young postmaster in 1945. The Shell Creek office operated out of the Brinkley store. (Courtesy of Joanna Miller.)

ROCK CRUSHER. Buck Mountain resident Floyd Hayes operated a rock crusher from 1956 until the early 1970s in Shell Creek. The Blue Ridge Stone Company provided gravel to area road construction crews, including those who built US Highway 19E through Roan Mountain. While the three-lane road was being constructed, officials had to detour traffic through Hayes's property. He charged drivers 50¢ to pass through. (Courtesy of the Floyd Hayes collection.)

SHELL CREEK DEPOT. The Shell Creek depot was constructed about 1882 along the East Tennessee & Western North Carolina Railroad. This rare photograph shows an unidentified man sitting on the depot's porch. Local residents worked hard to have the depot constructed. After the railroad stopped coming through Roan Mountain, the Shell Creek Depot was dismantled, with the lumber used to build nearby houses. (Courtesy of Patsy Young Crum.)

Bus Williams Store. Bus Williams and his wife, Mead, lived in the Shell Creek community. He ran a service station just down the road from their home place. The popular station was located at the intersection of US Highway 19E and Buck Mountain Road, the current site of a veterinary clinic. This photograph was taken when the new road was constructed. (Courtesy of Linda Brinkley Morgan.)

Bus Williams and the Quartet. Bus Williams, pictured with his wife, Mead, joined Roy Isaacs, Frank Holden, and Levi Holden on a Tweetsie train ride to Johnson City in 1928 to perform during the Johnson City Sessions, a legendary audition session for Columbia Records. The Shell Creek Quartet arrived late, but they still performed two songs, "My Boyhood Days" and "Back Where the Old Home Stands." (Courtesy of Linda Brinkley Morgan.)

ROY ISAACS AND FAMILY. Roy Isaacs and his wife, Bessie, wrote hymns together. She wrote the words and he wrote the melodies. Roy joined the Shell Creek Quartet, a group of four young men from the Shell Creek community. In 1928, the group participated in the legendary Johnson City Sessions. He is pictured with his parents, Bert and Betty Isaacs. (Courtesy of Rebekah Hunt.)

BRINKLEY HOUSE. James Walter Brinkley Sr. built his home in Shell Creek around 1900. Brinkley and his wife, Bonnie Church Brinkley, were in the retail industry. He built his store in 1905 and sold groceries, clothes, shoes, and feed for farmers. By 1924, he had built a new store at the present site of the Roan Mountain Riding Company. (Courtesy of Linda Brinkley Morgan.)

TOM THE TURKEY. It must have been Thanksgiving at the Brinkley farm in Shell Creek when this photograph was taken. Pictured from left to right are James Walter Brinkley, Bill Brinkley, and Jim Brinkley with "Tom Turkey." Turkeys, hogs, cattle, horses, and mules have been raised over the years in Roan Mountain. (Courtesy of Patsy Young Crum.)

STOUT HOME. David and Lurana Hodge Stout lived in this pre-1850 log home in the Buck Mountain community. It is where men from Buck Mountain met in the 1860s to join Union scout Capt. Daniel Ellis, known as the Old Red Fox, who led them across the mountains to join Union troops. (Courtesy of Emma Ruth Shomaker.)

THE YOUNG FAMILY. The Young family stands outside of their home in Shell Creek in this photograph. From left to right are (first row) Sandra and Ann Young; (second row) Dorothy, Patsy, and Mae Young; (third row) brothers Ernest and Leon Young. Leon Young was a lumber industry inspector and worked locally for the Graybeal family. (Courtesy of Patsy Young Crum.)

WILSONS AT SHELL CREEK. From left to right, Jack Wilson Jr., Fredia Keller, Betty Jo Perry, and Doyle Wilson pose for a photograph in 1946 in front of the East Tennessee & Western North Carolina Railroad in Shell Creek. Jack and Doyle are the sons of Jack Wilson Sr. and Joda Johnson Wilson. The Wilson family resided in Shell Creek. (Courtesy of Juanita Wilson.)

THE SNIDER FAMILY. John Snider and Lula Cornelia Hardin Church Snider sit on a porch in this photograph. The couple married after Lula Snider's first husband, William Church, died. Church built the store and house at the corner of US Highway 19E and Shell Creek Road. The store continued to operate after Church died. Amelia "Mead" Snider, the couple's only child, obtained the property after they died. She married Bus Williams. (Courtesy of Julia Kodak.)

AT THE STORE. From left to right, Ted Hoss, Patsy Young, and Mary Lou Potter pose for the camera in front of the old Brinkley store in 1936. The Brinkley store offered many services, including a general store, a post office, a justice of the peace, a barber, and a dentist. (Courtesy of Patsy Young Crum.)

DRIVING IN THE MOUNTAINS. The Brinkley family of Shell Creek goes for a drive in this early 1900s photograph. When the weather was warm, the Brinkleys enjoyed cruising through the mountains with their automobile's top down. They took many road trips in this reliable vehicle. The Brinkleys owned and operated several stores in the Shell Creek and Elk Park area. (Courtesy of Linda Brinkley Morgan.)

UPPER SHELL CREEK. This photograph was taken in the Upper Shell Creek community of Carter County in the early 1900s. Several of the youths became prominent citizens in Roan Mountain. From left to right are (seated) Lawton Hoss, Evelyn Brinkley, Ruth Hoss, Lowell Ellis, and Wilma Buck; (standing) Bill Brinkley, Hilliard Shell, Brady Ellis, teacher J.C. Wine, Erby Buck, and Zeb Graybeal. (Courtesy of Patsy Young Crum.)

FEEDING THE CHICKENS. Mary Jarrett Garland is seen here in the 1970s feeding her chickens. Garland lived in the Shell Creek community. According to her daughter Jeannie Perkins, Saturday evening was when the family killed the chickens for Sunday's meal. After killing the chickens, they would wash them and place them in the refrigerator. (Courtesy of Jeannie Perkins.)

PERRY FAMILY AT TEABERRY. This family portrait was taken in 1944 at the Perry farm in the Teaberry section of Shell Creek. From left to right are Roger, Dale, Ruth, Hyder, Astor, Louise, Jesse, Linville, Myrtle (mother), Lane, Geri, and Arthur (father). (Courtesy of Linda Perry Buchanan.)

THE ELLIS FAMILY.
Jennie Ellis, a single
and independent
woman, lived alone in
a small home at the
head of Ellis Hollow.
She had a cherry
orchard above the
house and liked to tend
to her garden. Family
members are seen here
at her homestead. Ellis
Hollow was named
for David W. Ellis,
who owned much of
the land. (Courtesy of
the Audrey Caraway
Julian family.)

MILLER HOLLOW BARN. Many memories have been made at this barn on Miller Hollow in Roan
Mountain, seen here in 1958. Children played hide-and-seek, people found love, and many stray
cats found a home in the barn, which remains in the Pippin-Ledford family. "I recall many nice
memories playing with Darlene Taylor and her brother as well as J.D. Burleson," said Jeannie
Pippin Grizzard. (Courtesy of Jeannie Pippin Grizzard.)

KILLING THE HOGS. Earl Pippin tends to the hogs in Miller Hollow. Raising hogs was a part of life. Hogs were usually killed on a very cold November day. After the killing, all went to work, rendering the fat for cracklings and lard, salting the meat, and hanging it in a smokehouse. The creek kept the meat cool, and the salt acted as a preservative. (Courtesy of Jeannie Pippin Grizzard.)

CLAUDE C. CHURCH. Claude Church is seen with his mule in Shell Creek in this early photograph. Church was the son of Lula Cornelia Hardin Church and an unidentified father. Claude Church was born in 1892, three years after the death of Cornelia's first husband, William Church. She later married John Snider. The Church and Snider families were in the retail business. (Courtesy of Julia Kodak.)

98

JACKSON GARFIELD POTTER.
Photographed in his uniform at the age
of about 19, Jackson Garfield Potter
of Roan Mountain enlisted in the
Army during the Spanish-American
War. Several men from Carter County
took part in the Spanish-American
War, including a handful from Roan
Mountain. Roan Mountain residents
have also participated in World War
I, World War II, and other conflicts.
(Courtesy of Andy Potter.)

LON HARRISON. Many people who
resided on Buck Mountain and in other
rural areas of Roan Mountain farmed
for a living. Lon Harrison, seen here on
the right with Jessie Harrison on the
Harrison property, was a lifelong farmer.
Lon later moved to North Carolina.
(Courtesy of Audrey Harrison Edney.)

HARRISON FAMILY REUNION.
The Harrison family of Buck
Mountain was large, prosperous,
and had many descendants. Family
reunions were cause for a wonderful
meal and spending quality time
together. James H. Harrison Jr.
is seen here at one of the family
reunions. The family would enjoy
a meal outdoors, reminiscing and
making new memories. (Courtesy
of Jeannie Pippin Grizzard.)

THE WILSON TWINS. Caroline and
Kate Wilson were born in November
1868 to George Washington Wilson
and Eliza Emmit Wilson, a full-
blooded Cherokee Indian. Both
Caroline and Kate were midwives
and lived in the Shell Creek
community of Carter County.
(Courtesy of Juanita Wilson.)

WILLIAM "BILL" GRANT. William Grant (1900–1965) spent the majority of his life in Butler, Tennessee, and in the Buck Mountain community of Roan Mountain. This rare photograph captures him in 1921, when he taught violin at Greeneville High School. Prior to teaching, he studied violin at the Cincinnati Conservatory of Music. Grant was a respected and talented man. The 1921 Greenville High School annual states, "Mr. Grant, although a very young man, has such a wonderful native ability in his art that he has no difficulty in satisfying the most exacting demands." In 1930, he married Maude McQueen. Following her untimely death, he married Lela Potter, a Buck Mountain native. Grant brought his fiddle to the mountains. Although he loved classical music, the locals preferred bluegrass, which he also played well. People still recall Grant and the beautiful music he played. (Courtesy of Dr. Rosemary Wolflin.)

SUNRISE VIEW CHURCH OF CHRIST. Sunrise View Church of Christ was established in 1903, and a building was constructed on Buck Mountain. It was originally known as Hannah's Chapel. Years later, the county obtained permission to hold school classes in the church. The building later burned, and a new building was opened in 1941. (Courtesy of the Watauga Spinnerrette.)

LAUREL FORK SCHOOL. Newt Shell's class at Laurel Fork School is pictured here. From left to right are (first row) Henry Potter, Melbourne Norris, Avery Hopson, Eldridge Jones, Paul Hopson, and Claude Blackwell; (second row) Elwanda Norris, Geneva Potter, Lara Holtsclaw, Anna Lee Brewer, Gladys Norris, and Goldie Blackwell; (third row) Cleo Potter, Virgie Potter, Gladys Hopson, Selma Baumgardner, Meakie Potter, and Blanche Isaacs; (fourth row) Dora Hopson, Lena Jones, Inez Holtsclaw, and Beulah Hopson; (fifth row) Bob Timbs, Jack Blackwell, Maynard Campbell, and Shell. (Courtesy of Andy Potter.)

Laurel Fork Church of Christ. First organized in 1882, the congregation of Laurel Fork Church of Christ built a new structure in 1943. Prior to the new building, the church met at a house and at Laurel Fork School. Some of the first members included Potters, Hopsons, and Kites. Preacher Robert O. Wilson is pictured here in the 1940s. (Courtesy of Andy Potter.)

High Point Church. Historic High Point Baptist Church is located on Buck Mountain Road near Laurel Fork. In this photograph, Virginia "Bug" Blackwell stands next to an unidentified woman in front of the church. Residents on Buck Mountain have several churches to choose from, including High Point, Buck Mountain Baptist Church, and Taylor's Chapel. (Courtesy of Andy Potter.)

MOONSHINERS. A legendary tradition in Roan Mountain, the manufacture, transportation, and consumption of moonshine has been a way of life for some residents. Here, two unidentified men are seen with bottles of moonshine. Locally, residents also call it "white lightning" and "mountain dew." Historically, illicit operations could be found throughout the Appalachian Mountains, including in the hollows of Roan Mountain. (Courtesy of Andy Potter.)

MOONSHINE STILL. Carter County law enforcement officers have located and confiscated many illegal moonshine stills over the past century in the Roan Mountain area. This photograph was taken in the early 1970s on Buck Mountain after the sheriff's department found an active still. Sheriff Harry Buckles (left) examines the still with deputy Jerry Weaver. (Courtesy of Keith Hart.)

EUGENE EDNEY. After joining the Marine Corps at age 17, Eugene Edney was on duty watching a military base gate when he met Pres. Dwight Eisenhower, who was recuperating after a heart attack. "He spoke to me and asked where I was from and shook my hand," Edney said. "I told him 'Roan Mountain, Tennessee,' and he said 'I know where that is.' " (Courtesy of Audrey Harrison Edney.)

CLIFTON SHELL. Roan Mountain resident Clifton Shell served in the European Theater during World War II. He received a purple heart as a result of his service. While participating in the Battle of the Bulge, he was wounded in the left ear and neck. During that time, his unit captured eight men. (Courtesy of Audrey Harrison Edney.)

105

RICHARD JOHNSON. Richard Johnson and Lawrence Pippin, lifelong friends, signed up for the Air Force on the same day, side by side, in 1962. Johnson served from 1962 to 1966 in the 325th Air Police Squadron, stationed at McCord Air Force Base. Pippin made the Air Force his career, and they remained the closest of friends. (Courtesy of Ellen Johnson and Jeannie Pippin Grizzard.)

BYNUM NORRIS. Bynum Norris showcases his corn cache at his home on Buck Mountain. Norris raised cattle, hogs, and chickens. He also had a small gristmill on his property and ground corn and wheat. Norris, a teacher and deacon at High Point Baptist Church, also worked as a cook at the lumber camps and worked construction, assisting with building the rayon factories at Elizabethton. (Courtesy of Harvey Norris.)

APPLE BUTTER. The old-time autumn tradition of making apple butter outdoors is captured in this 1971 photograph taken in Miller Hollow. Earl and Agnes Pippin, or "Pawdee and Granny," make apple butter in a large kettle as Lisa and Jeannie Pippin play nearby. (Courtesy of Jeannie Pippin Grizzard.)

GRANNY'S BIRTHDAY. The Grant family celebrates Granny Grant's birthday in this 1971 photograph taken in Miller Hollow. From left to right are Peggy Grant Pippin, Lisa Pippin, Lela Potter "Granny" Grant, and Donald Grant. Donald is petting granny on the head, which he did in a loving way while calling her "Jackson" or "Jackie." She looked like her father, Jackson Potter. (Courtesy of Jeannie Pippin Grizzard.)

WILSON FAMILY. The Wilson family is seen at left at their home on Bluegrass Road in 1937. Sitting outside the home are, from left to right, (first row) Doyle Wilson, Verl Wilson, and Jack Wilson Jr.; (second row) Jack Wilson Sr., Joda Johnson Wilson, and Celestine Wilson. Jack Wilson Sr. was a noted fisherman. In 1953, Jack and Joda Wilson moved to Johnson County, where they operated the Roan Creek Restaurant and Motel. Below, in 1959, Jack Wilson Sr. caught a 32-inch, 12-pound-10-ounce rainbow trout out of Doe Creek, which held Tennessee records for many years. (Both courtesy of Juanita Wilson.)

CASKET ON THE LAWN. An old-time tradition is seen in this photograph. An unidentified group of family and friends mourns the loss of a small child, whose casket is placed on the front lawn of this Roan Mountain house. This was a normal event in past decades, when families would place their loved one's casket outside for all to see and mourn. (Courtesy of Audrey Harrison Edney.)

CAMPBELL GROCERY. Campbell Grocery was located at the intersection of Walnut Mountain and Buck Mountain Roads in Roan Mountain. It was operated by Loanas Campbell. He sold a variety of groceries and staples, as well as cigarettes and tobacco. Harvey Norris said if Buck Mountain residents needed something they would go to Campbell Grocery or Blackwell's Store. (Courtesy of Harvey Norris.)

EZEKIEL POTTER. Ezekiel A. Potter was born on April 29, 1850, to John M. and Matilda McIntosh Potter. His grandfather John Potter, who was one of the pioneer settlers of what later became Carter County, Tennessee, died in Washington County, North Carolina, in 1789. Ezekiel married Delilah Messer, who was a Cocke County, Tennessee, native. He was an ordained minister of the Christian church, and served as pastor and held revivals in several small churches in Carter County, Tennessee, and Avery County, North Carolina. "Preacher Zeke," as he was called, was said to have been very active and very nimble of foot. Ham Potter told a story of how he skipped across a creek on a foot log shortly before he died, on February 25, 1943. He and Delilah are buried in the Isaacs Cemetery on Buck Mountain. (Courtesy of Andy Potter.)

JONES FAMILY. This photograph was taken of the Robert T. Jones family in 1905. They were one of Buck Mountain's first families. Robert Jones worked in a sawmill, according to his death certificate. From left to right are (first row) Lealer Banner Jones, Lura Jones Cordelle, Robert B. Jones, and Robert T. Jones; (second row) Henry Jones, Laura Belle Jones Potter, and Walter Lee Jones. (Courtesy of Andy Potter.)

LAWRENCE "TWEET" PIPPIN. Lawrence "Tweet" Pippin (1943–2010) was born and raised in Roan Mountain and became a career military man, serving in Vietnam. The only son of Earl and Agnes Potter Pippin, he is seen here in 1955 in front of his home in Miller Hollow. He remained in contact with his Roan Mountain friends and family, especially his lifelong best friend, Richard Johnson. (Courtesy of Jeannie Pippin Grizzard.)

COUSINS ON THE CREEK. Roan Mountain cousins Agnes Potter, Amanda Potter, and Hazel Stout are seen in this 1922 photograph, taken along a stream in the Shell Creek community. The Stout and Potter families of Buck Mountain and Shell Creek lived close to each other. (Courtesy of Jeannie Pippin Grizzard.)

DONALD GRANT. Donald Garfield Grant served in the Army during the Vietnam War. He was part of the 25th Infantry Division and the 4th Infantry Division, two divisions that experienced heavy combat and loss of life. Grant received several medals, including three battle stars, a bronze star, and a silver star, an honor for combat bravery. (Courtesy of Jeannie Pippin Grizzard.)

Five

RIPSHIN TO CRABTREE

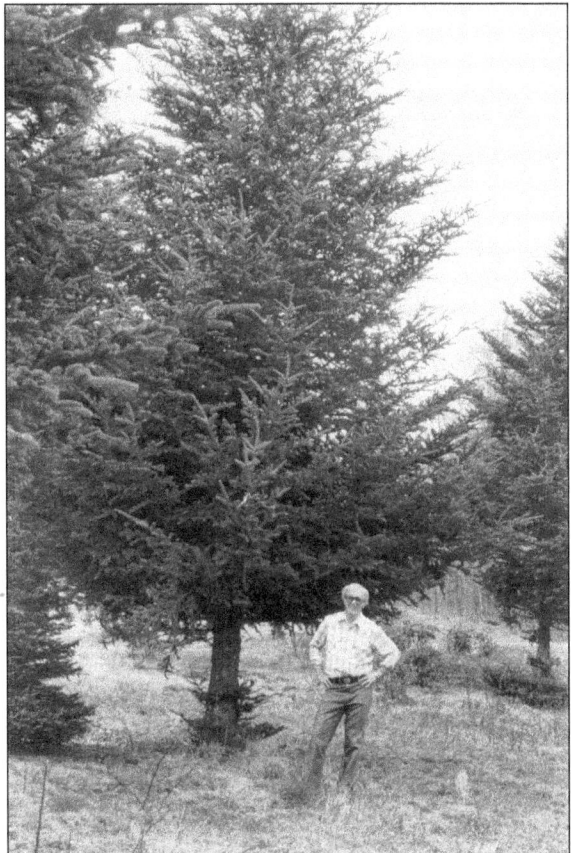

A.E. MILLER. The Christmas tree industry did not begin in Roan Mountain until 1954, when Dr. A.E. Miller, an Elizabethton dentist, and his friend Paul Foreman started the Ripshin Tree Farm at Ripshin Lake. Dr. Miller (seen here) planted Fraser fir, white pine, Norway spruce, Serbian spruce, and other plants. (Courtesy of Keith Hart.)

BOWLING CHAPEL METHODIST CHURCH. The Bowling Chapel Methodist Church, one of the predecessors to the Roan Mountain United Methodist Church, is believed to be more than 100 years old. The white clapboard building has also served as a schoolhouse, according to local residents. A tragedy occurred here in the 1920s when the song leader was shot to death in the church. (Courtesy of the Watauga Spinnerette.)

SUNRISE FREEWILL BAPTIST CHURCH. The congregation of Sunrise Freewill Baptist Church enjoyed taking trips in the Roan Mountain community. They are seen here in the 1950s. Families who have attended the church include the Simerlys, Arnetts, Chambers, and Millers. There are several small historical churches located in the Tiger Creek community. (Courtesy of Judy Guinn.)

OLD TIGER VALLEY SCHOOL. The original clapboard-sided Tiger Valley School was constructed in 1919. The school was named after James "Tiger" Whitehead, the legendary bear hunter who lived nearby. By 1936, the Works Progress Administration, a Depression-era federal agency, built a new rock schoolhouse to replace the clapboard building. (Courtesy of Greg Whitehead.)

TIGER VALLEY CHAMPS. In 1961, the Tiger Valley School boys' basketball team came in third in a tournament. Coach John Orr, seen in the first row, said he remembers the team beating a school in Unicoi County. Orr taught classes and coached the basketball team for several years at Tiger Valley before he went to work at Cloudland High School. (Courtesy of John and Phyllis Orr.)

TIGER VALLEY CLASSES. Students of all ages attended Tiger Valley School, an educational institute located about halfway between Roan Mountain and Hampton along US Highway 19E. At the time these photographs were taken in the 1920s, the school was constructed of clapboard. It was later replaced by the rock schoolhouse that is still standing today. The teacher, standing on the right side of both photographs, is Evelyn Young, who taught classes for several years at the school. After leaving the school, Young later became the postmaster in Shell Creek. She was appointed postmaster by Pres. Franklin D. Roosevelt. (Both courtesy of Patsy Young Crum.)

CRABTREE SCHOOL. The old Crabtree School, seen here in the 1940s, was constructed about 1929. Teachers at the small, two-room schoolhouse included John Morgan and Edna Potter. The school eventually closed permanently, and students began to attend Cloudland Elementary School. Tiger Valley School and the Hopson School were nearby. (Courtesy of the Elizabethton Public Library.)

HALL CHURCH. Tiger Creek's Hall Church is a large wooden structure built in 1890. Immediately inside the front entrance, visitors can walk into the first-floor sanctuary or go upstairs to the second floor. The first floor contains a piano, wooden pews, and an altar. A local chapter of the Odd Fellows, a fraternal organization, occupied the second floor. (Courtesy of Judy Guinn.)

JAMES "TIGER" WHITEHEAD. A Roan Mountain legend, James "Tiger" Whitehead killed 99 bears in his lifetime. While on his deathbed in 1905, Whitehead's friends brought him a bear to kill. They wanted him to kill his 100th bear. Whitehead thanked them but refused to kill the beast. He said he would only kill a bear in the wild, not one brought to him. He is buried in a small plot in the Tiger Creek community, which is named after him. His gravestone reads, "The noted hunter / James T. Whitehead / Born 1819 (Killed 99 Bears) / Died Sept. 25, 1905. We hope he has gone to rest." Country singer Johnny Cash wrote a song about Tiger after he was taken to the gravesite while on a Tennessee tour in the 1970s. (Courtesy of Greg Whitehead.)

BACKWOODS SCHOOL. The old Backwoods School was located in the Tiger Creek section of Roan Mountain on a dirt country road. Students would walk for miles to reach the small, two-room schoolhouse, built by Andrew Jackson Arnett and Amos Guinn in 1923. Buses did not run in the Ripshin area until 1936. In this rare photograph, the student body poses outside of the white-clapboard schoolhouse. In addition to the two large rooms in the schoolhouse, there was also a small cloakroom, which had two doors leading out onto the porches. The school, which closed in 1957, did not have indoor bathrooms, like many homes in the area, so students used the outdoor toilets. There was also no playground on the property, but students could play in the surrounding woods. There was also a field across the road where students were allowed to play. (Courtesy of Joanna Miller.)

CAPT. WILLIAM H. NELSON. Capt. William Henley Nelson, a Union officer in the Civil War, moved to the Ripshin Mountain area of Carter County around 1890. His historical farmhouse still stands near Ripshin Lake. Originally from Washington County, he had been to Ripshin visiting family during the war. After his military service ended, he returned to Ripshin and purchased a 1,000-acre farm. Nelson went on to be an Army captain, a county judge, a state representative, and a farmer. A group of Civil War veterans is pictured above. Wilson and his wife are pictured below. (Above, courtesy of Esta Street Stevens; below, courtesy of Greg Whitehead.)

HOPSON COMMUNITY. The Hopson depot and post office was located in the rural and isolated Hopson community, along the Doe River between Roan Mountain and Hampton. It was operated by the Rob Lacey family on the East Tennessee & Western North Carolina Railroad. It had a water tank, and the train would stop for refills. Residents could pick up their mail, buy a few necessities, or hop on a train at the depot. The Hopson community had several churches and the Hopson School. In addition to Hopson, there were two other stops along the railroad between Hampton and Roan Mountain: Blevins and Pardee Point, both of which were also along the Doe River. Railroad enthusiasts say the area around Pardee Point is one of the most beautiful locations along the Tweetsie's route. (Courtesy of Greg Whitehead.)

EARL SIMERLY HOME. Linda and Denver Simerly play outside in the grass in front of the Earl Simerly home in Tiger Creek. This photograph shows the two small children on the lawn, clothes hanging from the clothesline, and the Simerly homestead behind them. Earl Simerly and his wife, Edith Arnett Simerly, had nine children. (Courtesy of Judy Guinn.)

RIPSHIN LAKE. Scenic Ripshin Lake is located in the Tiger Creek community of Roan Mountain. Now private, the lake was developed in the 1930s when the Works Progress Administration built a dam. The land was owned by Capt. William Henley Nelson, whose house still stands near the lake. The Backwoods community was nearby. (Courtesy of Judy Guinn.)

WHITE ROCK SHEEP. The Roan Mountain area has become famous for its grazing sheep. *Elizabethton Star* editor Fred Behrend captured this scene on White Rock, between Roan Mountain and Hampton. Sheep tend to graze the slopes and balds of the Roan, as well as White Rock and other area mountains. Due to its unique location, White Rock was home to a fire lookout tower. (Courtesy of Linda Behrend.)

PRISON ANNEX. Durward Julian and his wife, Audrey, talk to Tennessee governor Ned McWherter (right) at the opening of the Carter County Work Camp, an annex of the Northeast Corrections Complex in Mountain City. The Carter County complex, supported by Julian and other leaders, was constructed on Railroad Grade Road in Roan Mountain. The annex opened in 1986. (Courtesy of Durward Julian and family.)

BLEVINS BRIDGE. The historic Blevins Bridge crosses over the Doe River in the Blevins community of Roan Mountain. The structure, a pin-connected Pratt through-truss bridge, was built in 1889 at a different location and then brought to Blevins to replace a flood-damaged bridge. It was originally used by the East Tennessee & Western North Carolina Railroad but was converted to a road bridge at a later date. The 110-foot-long, 9-foot-wide bridge has only enough space to allow one vehicle to cross at a time. It was constructed by the Keystone Bridge Company of Pittsburgh. The bridge once carried the Tweetsie Railroad over the Doe River and has also been called Tweetsie–Doe River Bridge No. 3. According to the Tennessee Department of Transportation, approximately 50 vehicles cross the bridge daily. (Author's collection.)

Six

RURAL ROAN MOUNTAIN

COUNTRY ROAD. This scenic photograph was taken in the 1940s and shows the Roan Mountain countryside. The roadway, dirt in this photograph, is believed to be State Highway 143 between Roan Mountain village and the mountain, at the state park. The wooden home on the right has not been identified. (Courtesy of Tennessee State Library and Archives.)

VIEW OF THE VALLEY. The valley below Roan Mountain is seen in this 1963 photograph from the Tennessee Department of Conservation. It was taken from Roan Mountain. Visitors to the Roan can see several states, mountain peaks, and communities from the top. A historical advertisement from the old Cloudland Hotel reported that visitors could see 100 mountain peaks from the Roan. The most notable mountains are Mount Mitchell and Grandfather Mountain in North Carolina. Visitors can also see the Toe River Valley in North Carolina and the Doe River Valley in Tennessee. The Roan is also a notable location to view the sunset and sunrise. Cherokee and Pisgah National Forests have erected lookouts across the mountain. The most popular lookouts are located at Roan High Bluff and the Cloudland Hotel site. (Courtesy of Tennessee State Library and Archives.)

HAMPTON CREEK VALLEY. This scenic photograph was taken in the 1960s in Carter County. The Hampton Creek valley and the site of Roan Mountain State Park are visible. This community has historically been home to many farms, as shown here. Barns, farmhouses, garages, fields, and a dirt roadway can be seen. In the late 1700s, during the Revolutionary War, the Overmountain Men came through this community while traveling to South Carolina to fight at Kings Mountain. More than 100 years later, citizens began settling in Hampton Creek, where they built Gray's Chapel and several homes. It is also a significant bird habitat. (Courtesy of Tennessee State Library and Archives.)

Visit us at
arcadiapublishing.com

....

www.ingramcontent.com/pod-product-compliance
Lightning Source LLC
Chambersburg PA
CBHW050545110426
42813CB00008B/2261

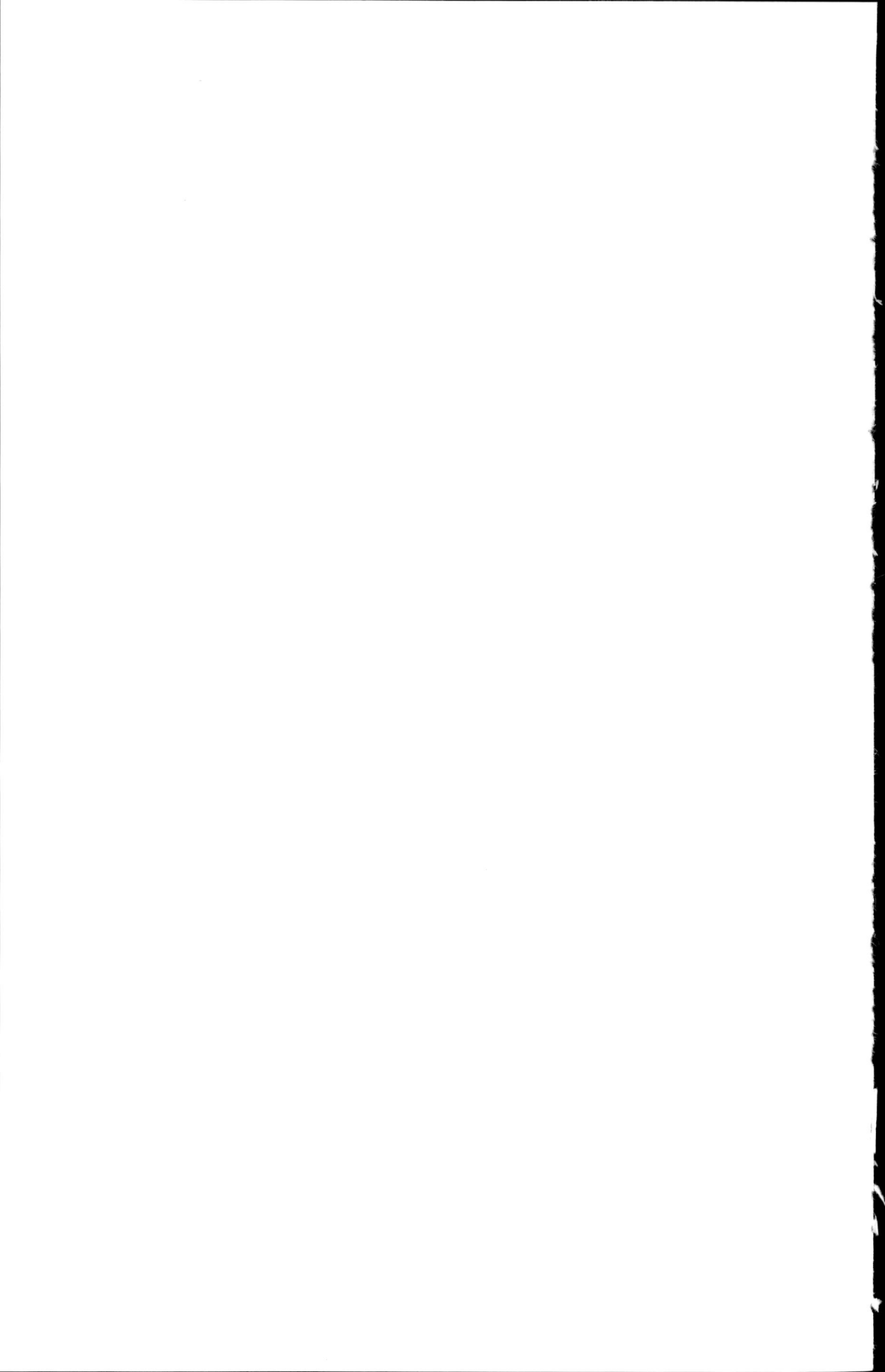